Japanese Economy and Society

— Key Terms and Issues

Mark Chang
Kazuhisa Horiguchi

SANSHUSHA

音声ダウンロード＆ストリーミングサービス（無料）のご案内

https://www.sanshusha.co.jp/text/onsei/isbn/9784384335156/

本書の音声データは、上記アドレスよりダウンロードおよびストリーミング再生ができます。ぜひご利用ください。

Download

Streaming

Preface

Japan, New Zealand, and Taiwan are the countries that I have lived in thus far in my life, and they are all intriguingly different economies and societies. This is why I have always been interested in these areas of study.

When I came to Japan to study back in the late 1980s, there were relatively few foreigners in the country. In recent years though, Japan has stepped up the pace toward globalization. The inflow and outflow of people and business activities have increased dramatically; therefore, we need to understand the Japanese economy and society in these contexts. We also need to grasp various economic issues which Japan is facing currently.

This textbook is basically an updated edition of *An Insight into the Japanese Economy* with more focus on technical terms. Like the aforementioned edition, it is written in simple English, and the contents are designed to be comprehensible for students without a background in economics. The textbook is intended to provide students with a basic knowledge about the Japanese economy and society while improving their English proficiency at the same time.

Mark Chang

まえがき

『英語で学ぶ日本経済とビジネス』の刊行から約 10 年が経過し、続編として本書『総合英語：日本の経済を知る・社会を見る』を刊行します。

日本の多くの大学生にとっては、経済のテーマは、日本語でも理解しにくいものです。本書では、大学生になじみのある経済事情的なテーマを中心に取り上げ、さらに巻末には「経済・ビジネス専門用語解説」を設けて専門用語について解説を加えています。

本書を用いて学習する前段階として、最近の世界経済や日本経済の流れをおさらいしておきましょう。2020 年に「コロナショック」が世界を襲いました。アメリカは「理由なき解雇」ができる国で、2020 年 4 月にはアメリカでは約 2,300 万人もの失業者が発生し、戦後最悪の 14.7% の失業率を記録しました。このコロナショックにより 2020 年の世界全体としての経済成長率はマイナスを記録しました。また、日本は失業率の上昇はわずかでしたが、2020 年の経済成長率はマイナスでした。

こうした異常ともいえる経済情勢に対処するため、アメリカ政府は現金給付を実施したり、インフラ投資などの財政政策を実施しました。またアメリカの中央銀行である FRB は、毎月 1,200 億ドル（約 14 兆円）の米国債等の大量買取り、量的金融緩和を実施しました。また日本も現金給付を行い、日本銀行は量的質的金融緩和の金融政策を継続しました。

この 2020 年の反動、景気刺激策の効果もあり、2021 年に日本を含め、世界経済は大きく経済成長します。アメリカの株価は NY ダウ、NASDAQ、S&P500 のいずれも過去最高値を記録しました。脱炭素による原油や銅などの資源価格の高騰、コンテナ運賃の高騰、物流やサプライチェーンの混乱、半導体不足などが問題となっています。アメリカでは 2021 年 12 月の消費者物価上昇率が対前年比で 7% の上昇を記録し、日本では多くの人が物価の上昇を実感するなど、デフレの時代からインフレの時代へと転換しつつあります。2021 年 12 月の雇用統計でアメリカの失業率は 3.9% にまで低下しました。FRB は量的金融緩和の縮小であるテーパリングを実施し、2022 年には利上げを予定しています。

コロナ禍にもかかわらず、中国経済は 2020 年、2021 年とプラスの経済成長を続けています。最近の中国の大きな経済問題は、中国恒大をはじめとする不動産業者の経営危機と不動産バブルの崩壊です。

振り返って日本経済を見てみると、トヨタやホンダなどの自動車やバイク、半導体製造装置、産業用ロボット、電子部品などの分野で世界的な企業はあるものの、世界的なベンチャー企業（スタートアップ企業）がほとんど生まれていません。アベノミクスには一応の成果があったものの、構造改革はほとんど実施できず、成長戦略を実行できていないといえます。賃金は約 30 年間上がらず、実質実効為替レートは 50 年前の 1970 年とほぼ同じ円安という「貧しい日本」「経済小国」になってしまったことを自覚するべきでしょう。

このテキストをきっかけとして、皆さんがさらに学習を進め、今後の就職活動や職業選択、経済生活、人生設計に生かしてもらえれば、筆者としてはこの上ない喜びです。

2022 年 1 月　　堀口　和久

Contents

Unit 1 Inbound Tourism
インバウンド・ツーリズム

インバウンド・ツーリズムとは、日本を訪問する外国人をターゲットとする旅行業という意味です。コロナ禍以前の 2019 年に日本を訪問した外国人の数は、過去最高の 3,188 万人に達し、旅行消費額は 1 年あたり 4.8 兆円にもなり、今後も日本経済の成長の 1 つの柱となることが期待されていますが、コロナ禍で日本を訪問する外国人は大幅に減少してしまいました。今後、インバウンド・ツーリズムはどうなっていくのでしょうか。

Vocabulary   01

Fill in the parentheses with the letter (A~J) of the matching definition.

1. insufficient   (　　　)   6. destination   (　　　)
2. accommodation   (　　　)   7. attain   (　　　)
3. friction   (　　　)   8. utilization   (　　　)
4. potential   (　　　)   9. dispute   (　　　)
5. atmosphere   (　　　)   10. municipality   (　　　)

A. 地方自治体   B. 宿泊施設   C. 摩擦   D. 目的地   E. 可能性   F. 活用
G. 雰囲気   H. 紛争   I. 不十分な   J. 達成する

From the standpoint of Japan, inbound tourists are foreign visitors traveling to Japan. Inbound tourism is one of the fastest growing industries in Japan. With a record high 31.9 million tourists visiting Japan in 2019, the nation seemed set to achieve its stated goal
5 of attaining 40 million visitors a year by 2020. However, because of the global outbreak of COVID-19, this momentum was disrupted.

Factors which have contributed to the industry's rapid growth in recent years include a relative drop in travel expenses for foreigners resulting from weaker yen, easing of Japan's visa conditions on
10 various countries, expanding operation of low-cost carriers, and an increase in the number of people—particularly in newly industrialized countries—who can afford to travel abroad.

A pressing issue which has come to light as a result of the growth of inbound tourism is the insufficient supply of accommodations
15 for foreign guests. The shortage of lodgings is especially serious in metropolitan areas. Utilization of private houses and apartments, known as *minpaku*, for accommodation will help fulfill the needs of tourists. However, as the number of tourists staying in such facilities increases, friction with the local community has risen
20 correspondingly. Because the *minpaku* lodgings are usually located in residential areas, issues such as excessive noise and improper garbage disposal by tourists can lead to unwanted disputes.

Inbound tourism has great potential to grow into a major industry of Japan. For some municipalities, it could even become
25 a catalyst for the revival of their local economy. If not managed properly, however, excessive inflow of tourists can ruin the charm and atmosphere of the tourist destination, and ultimately turn the tourists away.

---

from the standpoint of ~
〜の立場から見ると

weaker yen
円がより安くなったこと
low-cost carriers
(p.68 参照)
newly industrialized countries
新興工業国（NIC）

pressing issue
差し迫った課題
come to light
明らかになる

lead to ~
〜につながる

turn ~ away
〜を追い払う，〜にそっぽを向かれる

Exercises

A. Match the word with its synonym.

1. contribute
   a. contrive   b. help   c. contradict   d. prevent

2. facility
   a. establishment   b. agility   c. motel   d. facilitate

3. correspondingly
   a. contrary   b. sharply   c. matching   d. accordingly

4. revival
   a. rejuvenate   b. survival   c. revitalization d. destruction

5. ultimately
   a. absolutely   b. consequent c. eventually d. immediately

B. Read the following statements about the text and circle T (true) or F (false).

1. 31.9 million tourists traveled abroad in 2019.   (T / F)

2. One of the reasons for the growth of inbound tourism in recent years is the relative drop in the value of the yen.   (T / F)

3. There is an excessive supply of accommodations for tourists in city areas.   (T / F)

4. The *minpaku* lodgings are welcomed by all local residents.   (T / F)

5. The growth of inbound tourism will inevitably ruin the charm and atmosphere of the tourist destinations.   (T / F)

C. Listen to the dialogue and fill in the missing words. 🎧 03

A: Wow, there are 1.＿＿＿＿＿＿ ＿＿＿＿＿＿ ＿＿＿＿＿＿

＿＿＿＿＿＿ ＿＿＿＿＿＿ Kyoto these days.

B: I know, but some local residents are not happy 2.＿＿＿＿＿＿

＿＿＿＿＿＿ ＿＿＿＿＿＿ ＿＿＿＿＿＿ .

A: Why is that? I thought that the tourists would be welcomed by the local people

because they spend money and help to 3.＿＿＿＿＿＿ ＿＿＿＿＿＿

＿＿＿＿＿＿ ＿＿＿＿＿＿ .

B: Well, it seems that the city is under threat from the sheer number of tourists

visiting there, and 4.＿＿＿＿＿＿ ＿＿＿＿＿＿ ＿＿＿＿＿＿ and

noise pollution are starting to disrupt the Kyoto citizens' daily lives.

D. Below is the summary of the text. Rearrange the words inside the parentheses
in the correct order. 🎧 04

Inbound tourism has grown rapidly in Japan. Various 1. (costs / as / factors / such
/ resulting / cheaper / travel) from the depreciation of yen have contributed to
this upturn. The surge in the 2. (given / tourists / inflow / of / rise / has / to)
the problem of lodging shortage, and the number of *minpaku* has mushroomed as
a result. Although inbound tourism has considerable future possibilities, 3. (spoil /
tourist / mismanagement / attractions / can / the).

1. ＿＿＿＿＿＿＿＿＿＿＿＿＿＿＿＿＿＿＿＿＿＿＿＿＿＿＿＿＿＿＿＿＿

2. ＿＿＿＿＿＿＿＿＿＿＿＿＿＿＿＿＿＿＿＿＿＿＿＿＿＿＿＿＿＿＿＿＿

3. ＿＿＿＿＿＿＿＿＿＿＿＿＿＿＿＿＿＿＿＿＿＿＿＿＿＿＿＿＿＿＿＿＿

Discussion

Can you suggest some effective ways for municipalities to promote inbound tourism?

Unit 2 Corporate Social Responsibility
企業の社会的責任

経済学では，企業は利潤を最大化するように行動すると仮定されます。しかし，だからといって，企業は金もうけのために何をしてもいいわけではありません。生命や健康のように，お金よりも大切なものがあるからです。こうした問題は，企業倫理や企業の社会的責任（CSR）の問題と呼ばれますが，企業の社会的責任とはいったいどのようなものでしょうか。

Vocabulary   05

Fill in the parentheses with the letter (A~J) of the matching definition.

1. initiative	( )		6. investor	( )	
2. sustainable	( )		7. afforestation	( )	
3. development	( )		8. alleviation	( )	
4. stakeholder	( )		9. undertaking	( )	
5. depict	( )		10. transaction	( )	

A. 開発　B. 取引　C. 軽減　D. 取り組み　E. 投資家　F. 進取的精神
G. 利害関係者　H. 持続可能な　I. 描く，描写する　J. 植林活動

Corporate social responsibility (CSR) can be defined as a business approach that contributes to sustainable development by delivering economic, social, and environmental benefits for all stakeholders. CSR is a broad concept which addresses various issues
5 such as human rights, corporate governance, working conditions, environmental protection, cultural heritage preservation, and poverty alleviation.

human rights
人権
corporate governance
(p.69 参照)
cultural heritage
文化遺産

CSR is not a new concept in Japan. This term began to be used in Japan from around the 1970s, but in the early years, it tended
10 to be thought of in terms of philanthropic activities only. Going further back in time, the phrase *sanpo yoshi* (sanpo: three ways, yoshi: satisfaction) was used in the Edo Period to depict the ideal merchant spirit, meaning every commercial transaction should benefit not only the seller and the buyer but also the whole society.

tend to be ~
〜となる傾向がある
in terms of ~
〜に関して
philanthropic activities
慈善活動

15 Presently, many Japanese companies have set up specialized sections to carry out CSR activities. One of the undertakings which the Japanese companies are actively engaged in is the protection of the environment. This includes activities such as prevention of environmental pollution and promotion of afforestation.

set up
設置する
carry out
実行する
be engaged in ~
〜に従事する

20 Because CSR initiatives basically do not lead directly to profit for companies, it requires a strong will on the part of the management to sustain these endeavors. That being said, it is clear that companies can reap various benefits from engaging in CSR activities. For example, companies can improve their corporate image through
25 these efforts, which in turn may increase sales, attract more investors, and lead to recruitment of better employees.

profit
利益

that being said
それはそうだが

sales
売上高

A. Match the word with its synonym.

  1. benefit
     a. demerit **b.** convenient **c.** advantage **d.** detriment

  2. concept
     a. notion **b.** field **c.** conceit **d.** trend

  3. term
     a. terminology **b.** practice **c.** idiom **d.** terminate

  4. actively
     a. action **b.** passive **c.** keenly **d.** activity

  5. endeavor
     a. favor **b.** job **c.** initial **d.** attempt

B. Read the following statements about the text and circle T (true) or F (false).

  1. Corporate social responsibility is a business approach which aims to
     bring benefits to the whole society.   (T / F)

  2. The concept of CSR became well-known in Japan in the 1970s.   (T / F)

  3. In Japan, the roots of CSR can be traced back to the Edo Period.   (T / F)

  4. Many Japanese companies are actively engaged in prevention of
     afforestation.   (T / F)

  5. Companies which engage in CSR activities can derive various
     indirect benefits.   (T / F)

C. Listen to the dialogue and fill in the missing words. 07

A: I have to make ₁. _____ _____ _____ about the
   promotion of a particular CSR activity, but I don't know which one to choose.

B: How about the topic of child poverty alleviation? Did you know that about

   ₂. _____ _____ _____ _____

   _____ in Japan are living in poverty?

A: No, I didn't. But what ₃. _____ _____ _____ to
   reduce child poverty?

B: Well, for instance, corporations can help to ₄. _____ _____

   _____ _____ for children in need.

D. Below is the summary of the text. Rearrange the words inside the parentheses
in the correct order. 08

Corporate social responsibility (CSR) is a business approach that promotes
sustainable development ₁. (whole / the / benefit / of / society / the / for). In
Japan, the ₂. (traced / of / CSR / be / can / back / roots) as far as the Edo
Period, where a similar concept of ideal merchant spirit existed. Nowadays, many
Japanese firms have established specialized sections to engage in CSR activities
₃. (they / because / realize / can / they / derive / that) various benefits in the long
term.

1. _____

2. _____

3. _____

Discussion

If you were in charge of initiating CSR activities in a company, what kind of project would
you like to challenge?

Unit 3 Aging Society
高齢化する社会

高齢者人口つまり 65 歳以上の人口が，全人口に対し 7% を超えると「高齢化社会」，14%を超えると「高齢社会」，21% を超えると「超高齢社会」と呼ばれます。2020 年 9 月時点で，日本の高齢化率は世界最高の 28.7%であり，約 3,617 万人の高齢者がいます。少子化と高齢化が急速に進む日本では，今後どのような問題が生じるでしょうか。

Vocabulary   09

Fill in the parentheses with the letter (A~J) of the matching definition.

1. ratio ( )　　　6. scheme ( )
2. address ( )　　　7. premium ( )
3. quarter ( )　　　8. insurance ( )
4. issue ( )　　　9. immigration ( )
5. arduous ( )　　　10. aging ( )

A. 制度，仕組み	B. 保険料	C. 高齢の	D. つらい
E. 対処する	F. 4 分の 1	G. 問題	H. 保険	I. 移民，移住	J. 比率

Japan is one of the world's most rapidly aging societies, with more than a quarter of its population aged 65 or above. This ratio is expected to rise to about a third by 2030.

As the number of the elderly in need of nursing care increased, 5 the mounting cost of caring for them has become a big social problem in Japan. In order to address this issue, the Japanese government introduced the Long-Term Care Insurance System in the year 2000. This system is a public insurance scheme which provides social care to people from the age of 65, who have been 10 officially acknowledged as those needing long-term care services at home or at care facilities. The scheme is funded in part by central and municipal governments, and in part by compulsory premiums collected from people aged 40 and older. Under this system, basically 90% of the cost of care will be covered by the insurance, and the 15 individual only needs to pay the remaining 10%.

Another issue which the Japanese government has to tackle is the shortage of care workers for the elderly. The duties of care workers are arduous, and yet their wages are low. It is not surprising therefore that the job separation rate is high for this profession. In order to 20 improve the working conditions of care workers, the government took measures to raise their monthly wages by about 10,000 yen in 2017. The government is also starting to lower the immigration barriers for foreign care workers to make up for the shortage.

The above initiatives would help to ease the shortage of care 25 workers, but it may not be sufficient. Hence, other measures such as popularization of nursing care robots should also be considered. Japan has highly advanced robotics technology which can be utilized in the eldercare industry.

be expected to rise
上昇することが予想される

in need of ~
～を必要とする

Long-Term Care
Insurance System
(p.70 参照)
public insurance
公的保険

care facility
介護施設
compulsory premium
強制的に支払義務のある
保険料

job separation rate
離職率
working condition
労働条件

immigration barrier
入国の際の障壁
make up for ~
～を補う

A. Match the word with its synonym.

1. rapidly
       a. gently   **b.** randomly   **c.** swift   **d.** quickly

2. acknowledge
       a. deny   **b.** recognize   **c.** wisdom   **d.** scrutinize

3. remaining
       a. expensive   **b.** remainder   **c.** leftover   **d.** survive

4. measure
       a. momentum   **b.** step   **c.** pity   **d.** estimation

5. popularization
       a. spread   **b.** introduction   **c.** popularity   **d.** creation

B. Read the following statements about the text and circle T (true) or F (false).

1. More than 25% of Japan's population is 65 years old or above.   (T / F)

2. The Long-Term Care Insurance System is a scheme which provides social care to people who are 65 years old.   (T / F)

3. All people aged 40 and older have to pay premiums for the Long-Term Care Insurance System.   (T / F)

4. The government is trying to increase the number of foreign care workers in Japan.   (T / F)

5. Nursing care robot is an example of robotics technology.   (T / F)

C. Listen to the dialogue and fill in the missing words. 🎧 11

A: I heard on the news today that the government is lowering the immigration barriers for foreign caregivers. Do you 1. _____ _____ _____ about this?

B: Well, I know that the government revised the immigration law to include the care worker visa as a new 2. _____ _____ _____ _____ .

A: Does that mean we 3. _____ _____ _____ _____ foreign caregivers in the future?

B: Yes, in fact I heard that our 4. _____ _____ _____ _____ several Filipino caregivers next year, so I'm going to learn to speak Tagalog!

D. Below is the summary of the text. Rearrange the words inside the parentheses in the correct order. 🎧 12

Japan is among the world's fastest aging societies. In order to deal with the problem of rising cost of 1. (ever-increasing / for / caring / the / of / number) the elderly, the government started the Long-Term Care Insurance System in 2000. Another problem is that the care workers are in 2. (present / supply / short / Japan / in / at). The government has taken various steps to solve this problem, 3. (may / but / be / measures / required / additional).

1. _____

2. _____

3. _____

Discussion

Which industries do you think would prosper from the aging society and why?

Unit 4 Empowerment of Women
女性の社会進出

日本では企業における女性の社会進出はいまだ進んでいないといわれています。2020年3月期決算の上場企業では，女性役員比率は7％に満たず，約5割（1,152社）の企業では女性役員がまだゼロとなっています。こうした状況は問題であるという指摘がなされていますが，政府はどのような取り組みを行っているのでしょうか。

Vocabulary   13

Fill in the parentheses with the letter (A~J) of the matching definition.

1. equality	( )	6. proportion	( )
2. enactment	( )	7. dwindle	( )
3. progress	( )	8. imperative	( )
4. survey	( )	9. commitment	( )
5. mandatory	( )	10. managerial	( )

A. 法律の制定　　B. 強制の　　C. 緊急の，必須の　　D. 約束　　E. 平等
F. 管理職の　　G. 割合　　H. 進展　　I. 調査　　J. 次第に減少する

Recently, the Japanese government has announced its commitment to achieving a "society where women shine." In point of fact, the concept of promoting gender equality in society is not new in Japan. Some notable headways made in the past include
5 the enactment of the Equal Employment Opportunity Law (1986) and the Basic Law for a Gender-Equal Society (1999). However, the progress toward empowerment of women in workplace has been slow in coming.

According to a survey conducted by Teikoku Databank Ltd. in
10 2018, the average ratio of managerial positions held by women in Japanese companies was only 7.2%. The survey also revealed that the ratio of female managers tends to be lower in large enterprises as compared to smaller businesses.

In an effort to speed up the progress of women's empowerment,
15 the Act on Promotion of Women's Participation and Advancement in the Workplace was enacted in 2015. Under this law, private sector corporations with more than 300 employees, as well as government agencies and local governments, will be required to devise and disclose their action plans to improve gender equality with concrete
20 numerical targets. However, the drawback of this law is that the targets are not mandatory, and there are no penalties for companies that fail to achieve their targets. And even though the proportion of women holding managerial posts is gradually rising, the government was not able to achieve its stated goal of increasing this ratio to 30%
25 by 2020.

When we consider the fact that the Japanese labor force is continuing to dwindle at a rapid rate, the ability for Japan to fully mobilize its "womanpower" is now an imperative issue.

in point of fact
実際のところ

Equal Employment
Opportunity Law
男女雇用機会均等法
Basic Law for a Gender-
Equal Society
(p.71 参照)

according to ~
~によると
Ltd.
株式会社，有限責任の

Act on Promotion of
Women's Participation
and Advancement in
the Workplace
(p.71 参照)
private sector
民間部門

labor force
労働力

A. Match the word with its synonym.

1. announce
   - **a.** declare
   - **b.** renounce
   - **c.** answer
   - **d.** publication
2. notable
   - **a.** insignificant
   - **b.** obscure
   - **c.** noteworthy
   - **d.** notary
3. reveal
   - **a.** admit
   - **b.** bring to light
   - **c.** review
   - **d.** conceal
4. gradually
   - **a.** slowly
   - **b.** continuous
   - **c.** abruptly
   - **d.** cautious
5. mobilize
   - **a.** rely
   - **b.** mobile
   - **c.** remove
   - **d.** bring into play

B. Read the following statements about the text and circle T (true) or F (false).

1. The empowerment of women has not made any progress in Japan.　(T / F)

2. In Japan, the ratio of managerial positions held by women is relatively higher in small companies.　(T / F)

3. The Act on Promotion of Women's Participation and Advancement in the Workplace was deliberated after it was enacted in 2015.　(T / F)

4. At the point of 2020, the ratio of women holding managerial positions in Japan was 30%.　(T / F)

5. The diminishing labor force is not an issue in Japan.　(T / F)

C. Listen to the dialogue and fill in the missing words. 15

A: I read in this morning's paper that the prime minister of New Zealand became the first world leader to attend the 1. _____ _____

_____ _____ with her baby.

B: Really? That's impressive! I've heard that New Zealand is very advanced in the

2. _____ _____ _____ _____ .

A: Yes, it is. In my country, it's only natural for husband and wife to

3. _____ _____ _____ of housework and childcare.

B: That seems like a 4. _____ _____ _____

_____ to follow. When I get married, I want to be an *ikumen*!

D. Below is the summary of the text. Rearrange the words inside the parentheses in the correct order. 16

The government of Japan is aiming to create a society of gender equality. Some 1. (to / made / up / noteworthy / has / now / progress / been), but the pace is slow. In 2. (of / quicken / to / the / change / order / pace), the government enacted a law in 2015 which obliges large enterprises and government organizations to formulate 3. (toward / impart / and / their / achieving / plans) gender equality. Because of declining population, Japan needs to utilize its female labor force to the fullest.

1. _____

2. _____

3. _____

Discussion

Are you for or against the idea of setting a quota for women on corporate boards?

Unit 5 Consumption Tax
消費税

戦後の日本では，シャウプ勧告の影響により，国税に関しては，所得税・法人税などの直接税中心主義が採用されてきました。しかし高齢化率が急激に高まり，年金・医療・介護などの社会保障のための財源確保の必要性などの理由から消費税が導入されたのです。消費税率は 10% に引き上げられましたが，世界的にみるとこの消費税率は高いのでしょうか。

 **Vocabulary** 17

Fill in the parentheses with the letter (A~J) of the matching definition.

1. consumption	( )		6. finance	( )	
2. emphasis	( )		7. susceptible	( )	
3. taxation	( )		8. fluctuation	( )	
4. redistribute	( )		9. recession	( )	
5. revenue	( )		10. purchase	( )	

A. 購入（する）　B. 変動　C. 景気後退　D. 強調　E. 収入　F. 再分配する

G. 消費　H. 課税　I. ～の資金を調達する　J. 影響を受けやすい

Consumption tax, also referred to as value-added tax in some countries, is an indirect tax on the purchase of goods and services.

For a long time in the postwar Japan, the emphasis of taxation was placed on direct taxes such as income tax and corporate tax. The
5 system of direct taxation has an effect of redistributing income from the rich to the poor; therefore, it helped to raise the overall income level of Japanese people. This system worked well for Japan during the years of high economic growth, as the tax revenues increased correspondingly with the enlargement of corporate and individual
10 earnings.

However, as Japan gradually moved toward the age of low economic growth, it became obvious that a new source of tax revenue was needed to finance the ever increasing welfare costs for its aging population. Consequently, a 3% consumption tax was
15 introduced in 1989. The rate was later raised to 5% in 1997 and 8% in 2014. An advantage of the consumption tax is that unlike a direct tax, the tax revenue is not very susceptible to economic fluctuations. In this sense, it can provide the government with a stable source of revenue. On the other hand, it is criticized for being "regressive"
20 because it tends to place more burden on people with lower income.

Compared to other advanced nations, Japan's current consumption tax rate is still considered to be quite low. In fact, the average rate for OECD member nations was about 19% at the point of 2018. Later, the Japanese government raised the consumption tax
25 to 10% in October 2019, but there is concern that the tax hike may reduce consumer spending and lead to recession, as it did in past occasions.

There is no doubt that any form of tax will always be unpopular with the public. Ultimately though, whether the tax can gain
30 approval from the public or not will depend on how well the government makes use of the money for the benefit of its citizens.

referred to as ~	～と呼ばれている
indirect tax	(p.72 参照)
goods and services	財とサービス
direct tax	(p.72 参照)
corporate tax	法人税
high economic growth	高度経済成長
welfare cost	社会保障費
in this sense	この意味で
provide A with B	A に B を提供する
regressive	逆進的な
OECD	(p.72 参照)
tax hike	増税，消費税率の引き上げ
consumer spending	消費支出
make use of ~	～を使用する

Exercises

A. Match the word with its synonym.

1. enlargement
   a. engagement   **b.** diminution   **c.** expansion   **d.** distribute

2. consequently
   a. incidentally   **b.** with regard to   **c.** conversely   **d.** as a result

3. burden
   a. responsible   **b.** oppress   **c.** strain   **d.** encumber

4. unpopular
   a. farewell   **b.** disliked   **c.** populous   **d.** argument

5. approval
   a. empathy   **b.** acceptance   **c.** refusal   **d.** ratify

B. Read the following statements about the text and circle T (true) or F (false).

1. Consumption tax, unlike value-added tax, is an example of indirect tax. (T / F)

2. The system of direct taxation redistributes income to wealthy people. (T / F)

3. One of the reasons for the introduction of the consumption tax is to finance the rising welfare costs. (T / F)

4. Consumption tax tends to place more burden on people with lower income. (T / F)

5. The Japanese government is cautious about raising consumption tax rate because it had led to recession in the past. (T / F)

C. Listen to the dialogue and fill in the missing words. 🎧 19

A: These days, 1. _____ _____ _____ is really worried about the anticipated drop in consumption after the hike in the consumption tax.

B: 2. _____ _____ _____ raising the consumption tax is basically the same thing as raising the prices of goods.

A: Apparently, the government is trying to 3. _____ _____ _____ _____ of the tax hike by pumping money into the economy.

B: That might help, but if people continue to have a 4. _____ _____ _____ the future, then we can't expect a consumption boom.

D. Below is the summary of the text. Rearrange the words inside the parentheses in the correct order. 🎧 20

Consumption tax is an indirect tax levied on goods and services. During the postwar high economic growth years, the system of direct taxation worked well for Japan. But 1. (the / growth / down / slowed / as), the government introduced a 3% consumption tax in 1989 as a new form of taxation. Since then, the consumption tax 2. (stages / been / has / raised / in / gradually). Whether or 3. (accept / the / public / will / hike / the / tax / not) will depend on how wisely the government uses the tax revenue.

1. _____

2. _____

3. _____

Discussion

Would you prefer the government to put more emphasis on direct taxation or indirect taxation?

Unit 6 Deregulation
規制緩和

日本では，航空運賃の自由化による格安航空券の登場や，株式売買委託手数料の自由化，電力の小売自由化などの規制緩和が進められています。他方で，「岩盤規制」といって省庁や業界団体などが規制改革に強く反対し，規制緩和・規制撤廃が容易にできない規制もいまだに多いといわれています。今後，規制緩和の流れはどうなっていくのでしょうか。

Vocabulary   🎧 21

Fill in the parentheses with the letter (A~J) of the matching definition.

1. regulation ( ) 　　6. inefficient ( )
2. foster ( ) 　　7. criticism ( )
3. devastation ( ) 　　8. figure ( )
4. fragile ( ) 　　9. airfare ( )
5. hindrance ( ) 　　10. inequality ( )

A. 航空運賃	B. 規制	C. 阻害, 妨害, じゃま	D. 人物	E. もろい, 壊れやすい
F. 不平等	G. 育てる	H. 荒廃, 廃墟	I. 批判	J. 非効率な

Japanese economy is controlled by many regulations. These regulations were originally created to protect and foster the domestic industries after the devastation of the Second World War. The idea was to regulate the private sector so that companies won't be subject
5 to excessive competition while their business foundations were still fragile.

> be subject to ~
> ~に左右される，さらされる
> excessive competition
> 過当競争

However, as the economy developed, these regulations became a hindrance to new economic activities. Many industries, protected by regulations, became inefficient and uncompetitive. The regulations
10 also became a target of criticism from foreign countries that saw them as barriers to enter the Japanese market. Responding to the above developments, the government of Japan started to deregulate the industries gradually from the 1980s onward.

> uncompetitive
> 競争力がない

A notable figure in Japan's drive toward deregulation is
15 Yoshihiko Miyauchi, the former CEO of Orix Corp. His fervent devotion to regulatory reform has earned him the nickname "Mr. Deregulation." Miyauchi served as president of the Council for Promoting Regulatory Reform, and he asserted that regulations were hindering the freedom of business activities. He also pointed out the
20 difficulty of enforcing deregulation in certain sectors such as labor and agriculture, which are protected by powerful interest groups.

> regulatory reform
> 規制改革
> Council for Promoting
> Regulatory Reform
> (p.73 参照)

> interest group
> (p.73 参照)

Although the issue of deregulation is subject to fierce debate, from the point of view of consumers, deregulation measures can bring benefits in the form of lower prices and better quality products
25 and services. For example, the deregulation of Japan's airline industry has brought about a great increase in competition, resulting in a substantial reduction of airfares in recent years. However, some people argue that deregulation measures, especially those that are labor-related, can lead to widening of social inequality.

> deregulation measures
> 規制緩和措置

> social inequality
> 社会的格差

A. Match the word with its synonym.

1. foundation

 a. footing **b.** establish **c.** flounder **d.** dissolution

2. fervent

 a. apathetic **b.** enthusiasm **c.** ardent **d.** response

3. assert

 a. attack **b.** insistence **c.** claim **d.** convince

4. fierce

 a. constant **b.** fearless **c.** mild **d.** intense

5. substantial

 a. considerable **b.** worthless **c.** consideration **d.** abstract

B. Read the following statements about the text and circle T (true) or F (false).

1. Many regulations were introduced in the postwar years to encourage competition. (T / F)

2. The regulations were generally welcomed by foreign countries. (T / F)

3. Yoshihiko Miyauchi was a fervent advocator of regulatory measures. (T / F)

4. Excessive regulations can exert a negative influence on the freedom of business activities. (T / F)

5. There is an indirect connection between the deregulation measures and the recent drop in airfares. (T / F)

C. Listen to the dialogue and fill in the missing words. 📻 23

A: Why are there so many gas and 1. _____ _____

_____ _____ ?

B: That's because the gas and power markets are now fully deregulated. Previously, people had to buy gas and power from 2. _____ _____

_____ .

A: Well, I guess the 3. _____ _____ _____

_____ is a good thing, but with so many options to choose from, it can be a bit confusing.

B: That's why we should 4. _____ _____ _____

_____ _____ and not make a hasty decision.

D. Below is the summary of the text. Rearrange the words inside the parentheses in the correct order. 📻 24

Japan's economy is governed by numerous regulations 1. (the / put / were / after / place / war / in / that) to protect its industries. However, as time progressed, 2. (effects / to / regulations / negative / exert / these / began) to the economy and pushed the government to embark on deregulation measures. Deregulation is welcomed by consumers because they can reap various benefits from it, including lower commodity prices. But there is also 3. (that / deregulation / widen / concern / may / labor-related) social inequality.

1. _____

2. _____

3. _____

Discussion

What are the possible impacts of labor market deregulation?

Unit 7 Official Development Assistance
政府開発援助

世界には貧しい国と豊かな国があります。先進国の政府が開発途上国に対しておこなう資金や技術の協力を政府開発援助といいます。政府開発援助は役に立ってきたという意見もあれば，軍事に使われたりして有害という見解もあります。今後，世界の ODA はどうなっていくのでしょうか。また日本の開発援助政策はどうあるべきなのでしょうか。

Vocabulary   25

Fill in the parentheses with the letter (A~J) of the matching definition.

1. aid	(	)	6. steer	(	)
2. welfare	(	)	7. implement	(	)
3. organization	(	)	8. appropriate	(	)
4. infrastructure	(	)	9. bilaterally	(	)
5. springboard	(	)	10. multilaterally	(	)

A. 援助　　B. 組織，機関，団体　　C. 社会資本　　D. 割り当てる　　E. 二国間で
F. 実施する　　G. 誘導する，導く　　H. 福祉　　I. 多国間で　　J. 踏み台

Official development assistance (ODA) is defined as government aid that promotes and specifically targets the economic development and welfare of developing countries. Aid can come in the form of grants, loans, and technical assistance. It may be provided bilaterally
5 to a specific country or multilaterally through an international organization such as the United Nations or the World Bank.

The OECD keeps and updates the list of developing countries and territories. Only aid to these countries counts as ODA. Moreover, in order to be counted as ODA, the grant element (GE) of aid must
10 be at least 25%. The grant element is a measure of aid's concession to the developing country. For instance, the GE for a grant is 100% because there is no need for repayment.

The history of Japanese ODA can be traced back to 1954 when Japan joined the Colombo Plan. After this Japan began to provide
15 government-based technical and financial assistance abroad. Japan also began to extend grant aid as a form of quasi-reparation to Asian countries which had suffered damage during the war. Instead of cash, the grant aid was paid in Japanese products and development projects, including construction of economic infrastructure such as
20 dams and roads. In point of fact it became a springboard for later operations by Japanese companies abroad.

Two key players of Japanese ODA are the Ministry of Foreign Affairs which steers policy and the Japan International Cooperation Agency which is responsible for implementing bilateral aid. Japan
25 appropriates its bilateral ODA mostly as highly concessional loans with low interest rates and long payback periods.

During the 1990s Japan was the largest ODA donor in the world, but its amount of contributions started to decline from the 2000s because of tough domestic economic conditions and mounting fiscal
30 deficits. It should be noted though that the degree of contribution is assessed not only by quantity but also quality. Perhaps Japan should focus more on the quality aspect in the future.

economic development 経済開発，経済発展

technical assistance 技術援助

World Bank 世界銀行

GE グラントエレメント

quasi-reparation 賠償に準ずるもの

Ministry of Foreign Affairs 外務省
Japan International Cooperation Agency (p.74 参照)

payback period 返済期間

contribution 供与，拠出
fiscal deficit (p.74 参照)

A. Match the word with its synonym.

1. grant
   a. generosity   **b.** donation   **c.** speculation   **d.** gratitude

2. specific
   a. general   **b.** particular   **c.** impoverished   **d.** various

3. territory
   a. geography   **b.** border   **c.** municipality   **d.** region

4. suffer
   a. agonize   **b.** inflict   **c.** suffrage   **d.** witness

5. mounting
   a. countless   **b.** tiny   **c.** increasing   **d.** mount

B. Read the following statements about the text and circle T (true) or F (false).

1. Official Development Assistance is targeted specifically toward newly industrialized countries.   (T / F)

2. Japan's ODA is always provided through an international organization.   (T / F)

3. Grant is ranked highest in ODA grant element rankings.   (T / F)

4. Construction of economic infrastructure such as dams and roads is an example of grant aid provided by Japan to other Asian countries.   (T / F)

5. The Japan International Cooperation Agency is responsible for executing actual bilateral-aid projects.   (T / F)

C. Listen to the dialogue and fill in the missing words. 🎧 27

A: You know, when we talk about overseas cooperation, we tend to think in terms of massive ODA projects, but I think 1. _____ _____ _____ activities are just as important.

B: 2. _____ _____ _____ _____ _____ . Can you tell me a little more about those activities?

A: Well, I know that under the JICA's volunteer program, a large number of 3. _____ _____ _____ _____ are dispatched worldwide to assist the local communities in various projects.

B: I think this kind of good deed 4. _____ _____ _____ from the public.

D. Below is the summary of the text. Rearrange the words inside the parentheses in the correct order. 🎧 28

Official development assistance (ODA) 1. (to / aid / government / promoting / in / refers) the economic development and welfare of developing countries. Japan started its ODA program in 1954 in the form of technical and financial assistance to developing countries. Japan 2. (in / contributor / the / world's / was / ODA / number-one) the 1990s in terms of quantity, but perhaps to 3. (the / on / quality / more / place / of / emphasis) contribution is the way of the future.

1. _____

2. _____

3. _____

Discussion

What qualities do you think are required to become a member of the Japan Overseas Cooperation Volunteers? What are the challenges faced by the members?

DEMAND SUPPLY

Unit 8 Microeconomics
ミクロ経済学

経済学は経済理論と経済政策と経済史に分けられるとされます。最近の経済学は，理論よりも実証研究を重視するようになっていますが，理論の基礎についてある程度は理解しておいた方がよいでしょう。近代経済学は一般に，ミクロ経済学とマクロ経済学に分けられますが，ミクロ経済学とはどのようなものなのでしょうか。

Vocabulary 🎧 29

Fill in the parentheses with the letter (A~J) of the matching definition.

1. behavior	( )	6. principle	( )
2. consumer	( )	7. quantity	( )
3. corporation	( )	8. determine	( )
4. supply	( )	9. function	( )
5. demand	( )	10. preference	( )

A. 好み　B. 決定する　C. 関数　D. 原則，原理　E. 企業

F. 消費者　G. 需要　H. 行動　I. 供給　J. 数量

34

Microeconomics is a branch of economics which focuses on the behavior of consumers and corporations in the analysis of an economy. One of the important principles of microeconomics is the law of supply and demand which explains the relationship between

5 supply and demand in determining the price of goods and services.

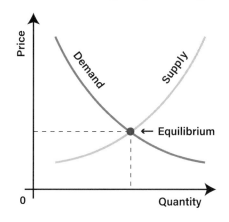

Changes in quantity supplied/demanded purely as a function of price are referred to as a movement along a supply/demand curve. On the other hand, a shift of the entire supply/demand curve is referred to as a change in supply/demand. Some examples

10 of factors which can cause the supply curve to shift include changes in production costs, changes in government tax policy, and technological advancement. Some examples of factors which can cause the demand curve to shift include changes in household income, changes in consumer preferences, and advertising.

15 Japan is a country which is heavily dependent on imported oil in the production of a wide array of commodities. Therefore, a rise in global oil prices will inevitably lead to an increase in the cost of production of manufacturers. This is an example of a factor which can cause the manufacturers' supply curve to shift upward and to

20 the left. Moreover, the government of Japan has been pressuring businesses to raise the wages of employees (thereby increasing household income) in recent years. This is an example of a factor which would push the demand curve upward and to the right.

law of supply and demand
需要と供給の法則
in determining ~
～を決定するとき

be referred to as ~
～とみなされる

production cost
生産費用
tax policy
租税政策
technological advancement
技術進歩
household income
家計所得

be dependent on ~
～に依存する
wide array of ~
幅広い～

Exercises

A. Match the word with its synonym.

1. focus

      a. concentrate   **b.** focal   **c.** experiment   **d.** transcribe

2. relationship

      a. specification   **b.** attach   **c.** enumerate   **d.** connection

3. purely

      a. simply   **b.** authentic   **c.** impure   **d.** solemnly

4. inevitably

      a. diligently   **b.** unavoidable **c.** naturally   **d.** circumstance

5. recent

      a. ancient   **b.** former   **c.** the latest   **d.** resent

B. Read the following statements about the text and circle T (true) or F (false).

1. Changes in supply and demand can affect the price of commodities. (T / F)

2. A general rise in the cost of raw materials can cause the supply curve to shift. (T / F)

3. A general rise in the bonus payments to workers can cause the demand curve to shift. (T / F)

4. An increase in global oil prices will work in favor of Japanese manufacturers. (T / F)

5. The Japanese government has been pressuring companies to raise wages because it wants to stimulate consumer demand. (T / F)

C. Listen to the dialogue and fill in the missing words. 🎧 31

A: Why is the government urging companies to 1. _____ _____

_____ of workers?

B: I think it's partly because they 2. _____ _____

_____ _____ to buy things to stimulate the economy and

tackle deflation.

A: How are the companies 3. _____ _____ _____

_____ ?

B: The response has been sluggish so far. If we consider the fact that many Japanese

companies now have 4. _____ _____ _____ , I

think they should share more generously with their employees!

D. Below is the summary of the text. Rearrange the words inside the parentheses
in the correct order. 🎧 32

In microeconomics, 1. (and / study / the / we / consumers / how) corporations
behave in the economy. A 2. (is / microeconomics / principle / key / of) the law
of supply and demand. Various factors can affect the supply and demand curves.
For example, in Japan, an 3. (in / prompt / oil / can / increase / prices) the supply
curve to shift to the left, and a rise in wages would move the demand curve to the
right.

1. _____

2. _____

3. _____

Discussion

Apart from the ones mentioned in the reading, what are the factors that would cause a shift
in the supply / demand curve?

Unit 9 Macroeconomics
マクロ経済学

マクロ経済学は，GDP，失業，インフレ，経済成長など私たちの日常生活と密接にかかわる分野を扱います。マクロ経済学の基本的な考え方は，世界大恐慌を時代背景として誕生し，イギリスの経済学者のジョン・メイナード・ケインズの考え方に基づいていますが，今後の日本経済・世界経済はどうなっていくのでしょうか。

Vocabulary 33

Fill in the parentheses with the letter (A~J) of the matching definition.

1. branch （　　）　　　6. anxiety （　　）
2. intervention （　　）　　　7. investment （　　）
3. unemployment （　　）　　　8. export （　　）
4. aggregated （　　）　　　9. import （　　）
5. equation （　　）　　10. nominal （　　）

A. 投資	B. 輸出	C. 等式，方程式	D. 名目の	E. 失業
F. 分野	G. 心配，不安	H. 介入	I. 輸入	J. 集計された

Macroeconomics is a branch of economics that studies the mechanism of an economy as a whole. Macroeconomics is based on the Keynesian theory which asserts that active government intervention in the market is necessary to maintain favorable
5 economy and low unemployment rate.

as a whole
全体として
be based on ~
〜に基づく
active government intervention
積極的な政府の介入
unemployment rate
失業率

One of the important aggregated indicators of macroeconomics is gross domestic product (GDP) which can be represented by the following equation:

$$GDP = C+I+G+(X-M)$$

10 In the above equation, C represents consumption, I represents investment, G represents government spending, X represents exports, and M represents imports. Each of these constituents can affect GDP which is a measure of economic well-being of a nation. For example, if private consumption (C) and business investment (I) decrease—as
15 in the case of a recession—then GDP will also decrease. To tackle this situation, the government may decide to increase its spending (G) or take action to promote exports (X).

government spending
政府支出

economic well-being
経済の繁栄
private consumption
民間消費
business investment
(p.76 参照)

Japan's nominal GDP was approximately 5.10 trillion USD in 2021. This makes Japan the third largest economy in the world after
20 the United States (22.94 trillion USD) and China (16.86 trillion USD).

USD
(p.76 参照)

In Japan, private consumption accounts for roughly 60% of GDP which indicates the importance of this component in the Japanese economy. Therefore, the government of Japan has been
25 deploying various measures such as easy money policy to stimulate consumer spending. However, the growth of private consumption remains low. This trend is particularly evident among young people, reflecting their anxiety toward the future.

account for ~
〜を占める

easy money policy
金融緩和政策

Exercises

A. Match the word with its synonym.

1. represent

    a. presentation   **b.** stand for   **c.** bestow on   **d.** stipulate

2. constituent

    a. nomination   **b.** component   **c.** equivalent   **d.** comprise

3. promote

    a. elevation   **b.** sell   **c.** encourage   **d.** impede

4. deploy

    a. use   **b.** exploit   **c.** plan   **d.** decoy

5. stimulate

    a. inspiring   **b.** arouse   **c.** enjoy   **d.** call for

B. Read the following statements about the text and circle T (true) or F (false).

1. According to the Keynesian theory, active government intervention is necessary to promote employment.   (T / F)

2. Tariff hikes on Japanese exports will have a positive effect on Japan's GDP.   (T / F)

3. A decrease in business investment on the latest technology will have a negative effect on GDP.   (T / F)

4. An increase in public works spending will have a positive effect on GDP.   (T / F)

5. The Japanese government has been trying to stimulate consumer spending by keeping the interest rates low.   (T / F)

C. Listen to the dialogue and fill in the missing words. 🎧 35

    A: Some economists are saying that Japan's public debt has expanded to

       1. _____ _____ _____ . Is this true?

    B: Well, for a long time, the government has been spending more than it taxes

       each year, so it is true that the debt 2. _____ _____

       _____ _____ .

    A: So 3. _____ _____ _____ is Japan's public debt?

    B: I read somewhere that it's more than twice 4. _____ _____

       _____ _____ . Fortunately for Japan, almost all of the debt

       is held domestically, so it's not facing foreign debt crises.

D. Below is the summary of the text. Rearrange the words inside the parentheses in the correct order. 🎧 36

Macroeconomics 1. (large / concerned / the / with / study / is / of / economic) systems. One of the main barometers of macroeconomics is GDP, and 2. (currently / third / is / Japan / biggest / the / world's) economy in terms of GDP. Because the private consumption accounts for a large proportion of Japan's GDP, the government has been implementing schemes to encourage the public to spend 3. (success / so / without / far / much / money).

    1. _____

    2. _____

    3. _____

Discussion

What are the fiscal / monetary tools of macroeconomic policy?

Unit 10 Balance of Payments

国際収支

日本の1人当たりGDPは世界で23位（2020年）とかなり下の方まで落ちてしまいましたが、まだ円は比較的強く経済的な豊かさを実感できています。これは日本の経常収支が黒字であり日本が世界最大の債権国であるためです。他方でアメリカは世界最大の債務国ですが世界第1位の経済大国です。これから日本の経常収支はどうなっていくのでしょうか。

Vocabulary   37

Fill in the parentheses with the letter (A~J) of the matching definition.

1. surplus　　（　　）　　6. liability　　（　　）
2. deficit　　（　　）　　7. stock　　（　　）
3. dividend　　（　　）　　8. bond　　（　　）
4. interest　　（　　）　　9. creditor　　（　　）
5. asset　　（　　）　　10. obstinately　　（　　）

A. 株式	B. 配当	C. 赤字	D. 債券　　E. 債権者
F. 資産	G. 利子，利息	H. 黒字	I. かたくなに，頑固に　　J. 負債

The balance of payments, also known as the balance of international payments, is the record of all economic transactions made between a country and the rest of the world over a set period of time, such as a quarter or a year.

5　　The balance of payments is divided into two broad categories. One category is called current account, and it records transactions such as trades of goods and services, payment of interest and dividends, and foreign aid transfers. The other category is called capital account, and it records purchase and sale transactions of
10 foreign assets and liabilities such as real estate, stocks, and bonds.

Japan has continuously recorded an annual surplus in its current account since 1981. Until the early 2000s, this surplus was sustained mainly by a hefty trade account surplus. In the past, this trade surplus has generated tensions between Japan and other countries,
15 particularly the United States which obstinately demanded that Japan should make its market more accessible for American products.

In recent years, the income account surplus has increasingly become a dominant source of Japan's current account surplus, while trade surplus has dropped. From 2011 to 2015, Japan's trade account
20 fell into a deficit because of a sharp increase in imports of fossil fuels following the shutdown of nuclear power plants in the aftermath of the devastating earthquake.

Although Japan's current account surplus is on a diminishing trend, it still has the most net external assets in the world, and the
25 country remained the biggest creditor nation for the 30th straight year in 2020.

balance of payments
(p.77 参照)

over a set period of time
一定期間

current account
(p.77 参照)

foreign aid transfer
経常移転収支
capital account
資本収支
real estate
不動産

income account
所得収支（第１次所得収支）

trade surplus
貿易黒字
trade account
貿易収支
nuclear power plant
原子力発電所

net external assets
対外純資産
creditor nation
債権国

A. Match the word with its synonym.

1. category
   a. classify   **b.** catalog   **c.** division   **d.** income

2. hefty
   a. feeble   **b.** exaggerated   **c.** wholesome   **d.** large

3. generate
   a. subside   **b.** generation   **c.** cause   **d.** delusion

4. accessible
   a. attractive   **b.** approachable   **c.** surge   **d.** comprehensible

5. dominant
   a. principal   **b.** secondary   **c.** conspicuous   **d.** submissive

B. Read the following statements about the text and circle T (true) or F (false).

1. The export of Japanese automobiles to China will be recorded in the
   current account.   (T / F)

2. Japan has recorded an annual surplus in its current account because
   of its strong export sector.   (T / F)

3. The United States thinks the Japanese market is easy to penetrate. (T / F)

4. Japan's trade account went into the black from 2011 to 2015.   (T / F)

5. At the point of 2020, Japan had maintained its position as the biggest
   creditor nation for 30 years in a row.   (T / F)

C. Listen to the dialogue and fill in the missing words. 🎧 39

A: I've noticed that the U.S. government ₁. _____ _____
_____ _____ _____ Japan to buy American
products recently.

B: I think that has something to do with the coming U.S. presidential election.
The President wants to impress voters ₂. _____ _____
_____ from Japan on the trade front.

A: Why ₃. _____ _____ _____ _____
before the election?

B: Because ₄. _____ _____ _____ can exert a big
influence on the outcome of the election.

D. Below is the summary of the text. Rearrange the words inside the parentheses
in the correct order. 🎧 40

The balance of payments is a ₁. (entities / transactions / statement / all / made /
of / between / in) one country with others. The balance of payments ₂. (basically
/ of / made / up / is) current account and capital account. Since 1981, Japan has
consistently recorded yearly surplus in current account, which had previously led
to trade frictions with other nations. Despite various setbacks, at the point of 2020,
₃. (as / Japan / maintained / the / its / position / had) largest creditor nation for
30 years in a row.

1. _____

2. _____

3. _____

Discussion

Which industries or products have contributed greatly to Japan's current account surplus in
the past?

Unit 11 Strong Yen/Weak Yen

円高・円安

1 ドル＝ 100 円の為替相場の状態から見て，1 ドル＝ 90 円が円高の状態です。他方で，1 ドル＝ 110 円となると円安ということになります。日本は「世界最大の債権国」であるため，日本円は安全資産とされ，リーマンショックや世界各地で紛争が起こったときなどのリスクオフ局面（リスク回避局面），つまり世界情勢が不安定になった局面では円が買われてきました。今後はどうなるのでしょうか。

Vocabulary   41

Fill in the parentheses with the letter (A~J) of the matching definition.

1. currency ( )	6. direction ( )
2. value ( )	7. appreciation ( )
3. correlation ( )	8. stability ( )
4. conversely ( )	9. coordinated ( )
5. tendency ( )	10. manufacturer ( )

> A. 通貨の価値の上昇，増価 B. 価値 C. 通貨 D. 協調した
> E. メーカー，製造業者 F. 傾向 G. 逆に，反対に H. 方向，方向性
> I. 相関，相関関係 J. 安定性

In the present day, most of the world's currencies are operated under the floating exchange rate system. Under this system, the value of a country's currency is determined by the foreign exchange market based on its supply and demand in relation to other currencies. This
5 is a sharp contrast to the fixed exchange rate system, where the rate is regulated by the government.

Along with other major nations, Japan also shifted to the floating exchange rate in 1973. Since then, the price of yen has fluctuated in correlation with various economic conditions. When the price of yen is
10 high in comparison with other currencies, it is referred to as a "strong yen." Conversely, when the price of yen is low in comparison with other currencies, it is referred to as a "weak yen."

Japan is a major exporting country, and basically, it has been a strong trade surplus country from around the 1980s. Therefore, there
15 is a prevailing tendency for the exchange rate to be pushed toward the direction of the strong yen. When the yen is strong, the Japanese exporters will suffer because the prices of exports will become relatively expensive for people overseas. And because Japan is a country which is heavily dependent on export earnings, a sharp yen appreciation almost
20 inevitably leads to recession. To avoid the negative effects of the strong yen, many manufacturers started to shift their factories overseas, which naturally led to the decline of production activities in Japan.

In 2011, the strong yen peaked at around 75 yen to the US dollar, but the tide began to change after the formation of the Abe Cabinet
25 in 2012. The following year, the Japanese central bank initiated a bold monetary easing policy. Keeping interest rates at record lows prompted the investors to shift from the yen to other currencies which can earn higher interest. As a result, the yen weakened to around 124 yen to the US dollar in 2015 and the export sector boomed.
30 Nevertheless, drastic fluctuations of exchange rates can exert a negative impact on the global economy, so countries should make coordinated efforts to maintain stability in the foreign exchange market.

---

in the present day
現在では
floating exchange rate
system (p.78 参照)
foreign exchange
market
外国為替市場
in relation to ~
～との関係で
fixed exchange rate
system (p.78 参照)

along with ~
～とともに
in correlation with ~
～と相関して

in comparison with ~
～と比較して

trade surplus country
(p.78 参照)

yen appreciation
円高

Abe Cabinet
安倍内閣

record lows
史上最低

higher interest
より高い金利

exert an impact on ~
～に影響を及ぼす

A. Match the word with its synonym.

1. operate

   a. administration   b. break down   c. manage   d. surgery

2. contrast

   a. contradictory   b. resemblance   c. contradiction   d. refute

3. prevailing

   a. prevalent   b. overcome   c. uncommon   d. premeditated

4. boom

   a. slump   b. flourish   c. bomb   d. whisper

5. drastic

   a. extreme   b. repeated   c. moderate   d. relentless

B. Read the following statements about the text and circle T (true) or F (false).

1. Under the floating exchange rate system, the value of the yen is determined by the government.   (T / F)

2. All nations of the world shifted to the floating exchange rate system in 1973.   (T / F)

3. When the yen is weak, the Japanese exporters will prosper.   (T / F)

4. In 2011, the strong yen reached its peak under the Abe Cabinet.   (T / F)

5. Volatile fluctuations of exchange rates will strengthen the global economy.   (T / F)

C. Listen to the dialogue and fill in the missing words. 🎧 43

A: 1. _____ _____ _____ _____ a foreign-
currency account at a bank.

B: 2. _____ _____ _____ . What made you decide to
do that?

A: Well, I 3. _____ _____ _____ _____
the ultralow interest rates of the ordinary deposit, and some foreign-currency
accounts are offering more lucrative rates.

B: I see. But you should be 4. _____ _____ _____
_____ _____ , because exchange rate fluctuations can offset
the gains made from interest, and you might even end up making a loss.

D. Below is the summary of the text. Rearrange the words inside the parentheses
in the correct order. 🎧 44

At present, the world is basically operating under the system of floating exchange
rates. Since its move to the floating exchange rate in 1973, 1. (of / experienced /
Japan / has / periods) strong yen and weak yen. A strong yen 2. (on / will / the
/ have / a / impact / negative) Japanese export industry—leading to economic
downturn. The price of yen was at its highest in 2011, but 3. (by / easy-money / of
/ since / introduction / policy / the) the Abe Administration, the price of yen has
weakened.

1. _____

2. _____

3. _____

Discussion 💬

What are the merits and demerits of strong yen / weak yen from the standpoint of the
Japanese economy?

Unit **12** **Mergers and Acquisitions (M&A)**

企業の合併・買収

少子化により学校法人の経営も大変な状況で，学校法人の買収や合併がニュースになっています。企業の買収や合併のニュースもよく耳にします。中小企業の後継者難などもあって，M&A の件数は右肩上がりに増加し多くの会社が M&A に関心をもっていますが，今度はどうなっていくのでしょうか。

Vocabulary   45

Fill in the parentheses with the letter (A~J) of the matching definition.

1. merger	(	)		6. objective	(	)	
2. acquisition	(	)		7. capital	(	)	
3. listed	(	)		8. accumulated	(	)	
4. shareholder	(	)		9. deal	(	)	
5. founder	(	)		10. prominence	(	)	

A. 卓越, 傑出	B. 資本	C. 取引	D. 合併
E. 上場している	F. 買収	G. 失敗する	H. 目標	I. 株主	J. 蓄積された

In the corporate world, a merger is the act of joining two or more companies into one. Meanwhile, an acquisition refers to the purchase of one company by another. It should be noted that in most cases, a merger is friendlier in nature than an acquisition.

5　　When a company wishes to purchase another company which is listed on the stock market, a method called takeover bid (TOB) is often adopted. In a takeover bid, a prospective acquirer openly proposes to buy shares from every shareholders of the target company for a certain price during a specified period, subject to the
10 tendering of a specified number of shares.

Backed up by low borrowing costs and ample accumulated capital, the Japanese companies have increased their M&A activities in recent years. According to an industry survey, "The number of mergers and acquisitions involving Japanese firms in 2017 grew 15
15 percent from the previous year to 3,050, rewriting a record high for the first time in 11 years."[*1]

In particular, the outbound M&A deals by Japanese companies are on the rise. In its report in 2017, JP Morgan Chase & Co. stated, "To regain global prominence with a shrinking domestic economy,
20 Japanese corporations must acquire market share by entering new markets or expanding into new growth areas. Relying purely on in-house R&D and organic growth from the domestic market alone is clearly insufficient to achieve growth objectives."[*2]

Possible merits to be derived from M&A include gaining new
25 distribution network and cost savings in research and development through rationalization. However, there are always risks involved in M&A transactions, and some deals may founder.

corporate world
実業界

listed on the stock market
株式市場に上場されている
TOB
（p.79 参照）
subject to ~
～を条件として

backed up by ~
～に支えられて

rewrite a record high
最高記録を書きかえる

global prominence
国際的優勢
market share
市場占有率

R&D
研究開発
organic growth
（p.79 参照）

distribution network
流通ネットワーク

*1 M&A's involving Japanese firms in 2017 set record high for first time in 11 years (The Japan Times, January 5, 2018)
*2 Global M&A activity is slowing, but Japanese firms are aggressively acquiring overseas (CNBC, June 21, 2017)

A. Match the word with its synonym.

1. meanwhile

   a. now   **b.** awhile   **c.** later on   **d.** in the meantime

2. adopt

   a. recommend   **b.** abandon   **c.** adoption   **d.** choose

3. tender

   a. offer   **b.** tentative   **c.** shed   **d.** tenderness

4. shrinking

   a. growing   **b.** diminishing   **c.** contract   **d.** sinking

5. insufficient

   a. impossible   **b.** plenty   **c.** unsatisfied   **d.** inadequate

B. Read the following statements about the text and circle T (true) or F (false).

1. A merger generally refers to a hostile takeover. (T / F)

2. In a takeover bid, a prospective acquirer proposes to buy shares from a limited number of shareholders. (T / F)

3. In recent years, 3,050 Japanese companies were acquired by foreign capital. (T / F)

4. The outbound M&A deals by Japanese companies are increasing because the domestic market is becoming smaller. (T / F)

5. An advantage of M&A is that there are hardly any risks involved in the deals. (T / F)

C. Listen to the dialogue and fill in the missing words. 47

A: I saw a tender offer announcement in a 1. _____ _____

_____ . I think it's a hostile takeover bid.

B: I saw it too. I was surprised because 2. _____ _____

_____ _____ hostile takeovers in Japan.

A: Do you think 3. _____ _____ _____

_____ ?

B: It probably won't go as planned. In the past, similar attempts have almost always failed. It seems that the practice of hostile takeovers doesn't 4. _____

_____ _____ _____ .

D. Below is the summary of the text. Rearrange the words inside the parentheses in the correct order. 48

A merger means combining separate companies, and an acquisition means purchasing another company. Taking advantage of favorable conditions, Japanese companies 1. (pursuits / up / their / have / stepped / M&A), especially in foreign countries. Because of a diminishing domestic market, there is an earnest need for Japanese companies to acquire new markets overseas or 2. (new / business / advance / of / fields / into). M&A can help companies achieve their growth objectives, and 3. (their / such / merits / provide / as / strengthening) distribution network.

1. _____

2. _____

3. _____

Discussion

Which Japanese companies have been actively engaged in M&A activities in recent years? Can you give examples of their M&A deals?

Unit 13 Individual Investors

個人投資家

急激な高齢化と少子化により，年金や医療などの社会保障があてにできない世の中になりそうです。したがって，証券投資などについてのファイナンシャルリテラシー（Financial Literacy），金融の知識を身につけておくことは重要でしょう。あなたは株式投資などの証券投資に興味がありますか。

 49

Fill in the parentheses with the letter (A~J) of the matching definition.

1. household	(	)	6. skeptical	(	)	
2. securities	(	)	7. inherently	(	)	
3. avert	(	)	8. reinvigorate	(	)	
4. exemption	(	)	9. launch	(	)	
5. expectation	(	)	10. trillion	(	)	

A. 有価証券　　B. 回避する，避ける　　C. 兆　　D. 開始する，始める　　E. 懐疑的な
F. 内在的に　　G. 期待　　H. 世帯　　I. 再び活気を与える　　J. 免除

The government of Japan is stepping up its drive to boost the public's appetite for investment. At present, about half of the financial assets owned by Japanese households are in cash or bank accounts. Only about 15% is held in investments, compared to
5 around 50% in the U.S.

Traditionally, Japanese people tend to be skeptical when it comes to investing in securities which they see as being inherently risky. Instead, they prefer to avert risks by keeping their money in savings accounts or as cash stashed away somewhere in their house.
10 However, some financial experts assert that, "Persuading Japanese to move their savings out of bank accounts and government bonds and into riskier assets is vital for reinvigorating Japan's long-sluggish economy and financing the retirements of its rapidly aging people."

One of the government's schemes to encourage investment by
15 individuals is the Nippon Individual Savings Account Program, or NISA. This scheme was launched in 2014 to attract individual investors by exempting holders of such accounts from the 20% tax on income from investments, including capital gains and dividends. The tax exemption applies to all returns from annual investments of up to
20 1.2 million yen made over a five-year period. Individual investors can open a NISA account at banks and securities companies.

According to the Financial Services Agency of Japan, at the point of March 2018 there was 13.9 trillion yen invested in NISA accounts, 58.6% of which was in mutual funds. The performance
25 of NISA in terms of the total amount of money invested in it so far has not met the government's expectations. It remains to be seen whether the government can come up with more innovative schemes to prompt the public to invest.

step up a drive to do ~
～する運動を進める
at present
現在
financial assets
金融資産
bank account
銀行口座

when it comes to ~
～のこととなると

avert risk
リスクを回避する
savings account
(p.80 参照)

government bond
国債，公債

NISA
(p.80 参照)

capital gains
キャピタルゲイン，売却
益

Financial Services
Agency
金融庁

mutual fund
投資信託

come up with ~
～を思いつく

A. Match the word with its synonym.

1. boost

   a. disembark   **b.** boast   **c.** enhance   **d.** obstruct

2. appetite

   a. antipathy   **b.** craving   **c.** appetizing   **d.** adherence

3. persuade

   a. persuasive   **b.** convince   **c.** dissuade   **d.** perceive

4. return

   a. profit   **b.** depart   **c.** loan   **d.** regain

5. performance

   a. stage   **b.** theatrical   **c.** accomplishment   **d.** formation

B. Read the following statements about the text and circle T (true) or F (false).

1. At present, about 50% of the financial assets owned by
   American households are in cash or bank accounts.   (T / F)

2. Traditionally, Japanese people preferred to keep their money in banks
   rather than investing in securities.   (T / F)

3. A major drawback of NISA is that it does not provide any incentives
   for the investors.   (T / F)

4. Currently, NISA accounts are mainly held by corporations.   (T / F)

5. The Japanese government is very satisfied with the performance
   of NISA so far.   (T / F)

C. Listen to the dialogue and fill in the missing words. 51

A: A friend of mine works in a securities company, and she 1. _____

_____ _____ me to buy stocks. What do you think I should

do?

B: You can give it a try. It's better than 2. _____ _____

_____ _____ _____ .

A: I 3. _____ _____ _____ _____ .

Anyway, I have to start building up assets in preparation for my retirement.

B: Yeah, a recent report estimated that 4. _____ _____

_____ _____ would need retirement savings of at least 20

million yen.

D. Below is the summary of the text. Rearrange the words inside the parentheses
in the correct order. 52

Currently, only about 15% of financial assets owned by the Japanese public is
held in investments. This figure reflects Japanese people's 1. (avoid / risks / to / in
/ tendency / related / to / matters) money. But in order to stimulate economic
activities, the government 2. (encourage / invest / to / needs / more / individuals /
to). For this reason, the scheme of NISA was initiated in 2014. However, this 3. (to
/ has / up / scheme / to / yet / live / the) government's expectations.

1. _____

2. _____

3. _____

Discussion

Do you think it is a good idea to start saving and investing for retirement at a young age?

Unit 14 Big Data
ビッグデータ

2011 年ごろからビッグデータが注目され始めました。これからの企業は，データ技術を活用できなければ淘汰されてしまうといわれています。IT 技術の主役は，クラウド・ビッグデータ，AI（人工知能），5G の 3 つであるといわれています。あなたはこの IT・AI（人工知能）の時代を生き残ることができますか。

Vocabulary   53

Fill in the parentheses with the letter (A~J) of the matching definition.

1. stream	( )	6. intelligence	( )
2. advancement	( )	7. unprecedented	( )
3. massive	( )	8. strategy	( )
4. structured	( )	9. optimum	( )
5. artificial	( )	10. anonymous	( )

A. 知能　　B. 巨大な　　C. 戦略　　D. 流れ　　E. 最適な　　F. 人工の
G. 匿名の　　H. 構造化された　　I. かつてない，空前の　　J. 進歩

We live in a world that is filled with data. In the past, there was no means to make full use of various kinds of data generated from our daily activities. However, thanks to the rapid spread of the Internet and the advancement of computer technology, we can now utilize massive volume of data, referred to as Big Data, to our best advantage in business and many other fields.

Big Data can be collected in a wide range of formats—from traditional structured databases to unstructured photos, videos, audios, emails, text documents, and sensor data. The ever-growing stream of data can now be analyzed at an unprecedented speed with the aid of artificial intelligence.

By analyzing Big Data, companies can improve their marketing strategies. It is now possible for companies to predict what specific clusters of customers will want to buy, and when, to a highly accurate degree. Big Data also helps companies to improve their operation efficiency and make optimum decisions speedily.

Although Big Data can provide tremendous future opportunities for Japanese industries, there are some issues which need to be addressed. Firstly, there is an urgent need to increase the number of data scientists who can deal with the complex analysis of Big Data. Currently, there is a serious shortage of data scientists in Japan. Another issue which is raising concerns is the matter of information management. Big Data contains a lot of information about our personal lives. Even though the pieces of information used for analysis are usually made anonymous, many people have a feeling of anxiety about the privacy and security of data. Japanese industries need to take appropriate measures to mitigate these anxieties.

(line markers: 5, 10, 15, 20, 25)

make full use of ~
~を充分に活用する

utilize ~ to one's best advantage
~を最大限に利用する

stream of data
データの流れ
artificial intelligence
(p.81 参照)

operation efficiency
業務効率

data scientist
データサイエンティスト
information management
情報管理

A. Match the word with its synonym.

1. means
       a. method   **b.** necessity   **c.** meaning   **d.** rationale

2. spread
       a. spray   **b.** settlement   **c.** speed   **d.** diffusion

3. format
       a. inauguration **b.** style   **c.** fortune   **d.** formal

4. cluster
       a. quest   **b.** age   **c.** group   **d.** clue

5. mitigate
       a. vindicate   **b.** aggravate   **c.** meditate   **d.** appease

B. Read the following statements about the text and circle T (true) or F (false).

1. The development of the Internet and computer technology has made
   it possible for us to use Big Data effectively.   (T / F)

2. Big Data only refers to traditional structured databases.   (T / F)

3. Big Data can help companies in carrying out prediction, operation,
   and decision making.   (T / F)

4. Currently, there is an excess supply of data scientists in Japan.   (T / F)

5. If Big Data is not managed properly, people's privacy and security
   could be jeopardized.   (T / F)

C. Listen to the dialogue and fill in the missing words. 🎧 55

   A: Hey, let's go to that new *kaiten-sushi* restaurant near the station for lunch. It's

      1. —————————— —————————— —————————— .

   B: Great! By the way, did you know that 2. —————————— ——————————

      —————————— IC tags on *sushi* plates to collect data on consumption patterns

      of customers?

   A: Yes, I know. I've heard that in the case of big *kaiten-sushi* chain stores,

      the aggregated pieces of data collected can reach a 3. ——————————

      —————————— —————————— —————————— in a year.

   B: 4. —————————— —————————— —————————— —————————— , we

      might have IC tags attached onto us!

D. Below is the summary of the text. Rearrange the words inside the parentheses in the correct order. 🎧 56

    The development of the Internet and the computer technology 1. (utilize / it / has / possible / us / made / for / to) Big Data in business and other areas. Big Data 2. (many / can / in / be / comes / and / formats) analyzed speedily with the help of artificial intelligence. Through the analysis of Big Data, 3. (administration / can / companies / enhance / their). However, some issues such as the shortage of data scientists and the security concerns need to be addressed.

   1. _____

   2. _____

   3. _____

Discussion

Can you suggest any new ways to make good use of Big Data?

Unit 15 Fintech
フィンテック

ビットコインのような暗号資産の登場，AI による信用スコアリング，キャッシュレス決済，ロボットによるロボアドバイザーなど，フィンテックの分野の技術革新には目を見張るものがあります。フェイスブックのリブラも世界を驚かせました。ドルや円といった通貨や金融ビジネスはこれからどうなってしまうのでしょうか。

Vocabulary   57

Fill in the parentheses with the letter (A~J) of the matching definition.

1. conservative	( )	6. payment	( )
2. obstacle	( )	7. indication	( )
3. daunting	( )	8. innovative	( )
4. entrepreneur	( )	9. settle	( )
5. coinage	( )	10. traditionally	( )

A. 造語（新しく作られた造語）　　B. 革新的な　　C. 決済する

D. しるし，表示　　E. 保守的な　　F. 伝統的に　　G. 障害，邪魔

H. 気が重い，やる気をくじく　　I. 起業家　　J. 支払い

Fintech is a coinage derived from combining the words "financial" and "technology." It refers to the use of information technology (IT) to provide various financial services and products.

Fintech is developing rapidly, and it is changing the world of
5 finance for the general public. For example, many payments can now be settled over the Internet. We can open a bank account entirely online, and we can link the account to our personal computer or smartphone and use them to keep track of all transactions.

In the world of business, fintech is also becoming a game
10 changer. One example can be found in the area of financing. Traditionally, one of the biggest obstacles for someone who wants to start up a new business is the daunting task of obtaining a loan from the bank. But thanks to the advancement in fintech, it is now possible for aspiring entrepreneurs to raise funds over the Internet by using
15 a method called crowdfunding. In fact, crowdfunding allows people with innovative ideas (but no money) to gather funds quickly and easily from a "crowd" of people connected to the Internet.

In Japan, fintech-related venture companies are growing in numbers, and fintech terminology such as virtual currency and
20 electronic money are fast becoming household words. However, according to a report released by the Bank of Japan, in 2017 each citizen in Japan possessed 2.9 electronic money cards on average, but only 30% of citizens used them on a daily basis. This is an indication that Japanese people still hold conservative views when it comes to
25 the means of currency usage.

derived from ~
～に由来する

keep track of ~
～の経過を追う，たどる
game changer
ゲームチェンジャー

crowdfunding
(p.82 参照)

virtual currency
(p.82 参照)
household word
誰でもよく知っている言葉

A. Match the word with its synonym.

1. combine
   a. fix **b.** split up **c.** amalgamation **d.** join

2. entirely
   a. thorough **b.** partially **c.** totally **d.** reasonable

3. connect
   a. link **b.** subscribe **c.** glimpse **d.** dissociate

4. release
   a. hand over **b.** relief **c.** detain **d.** make public

5. possess
   a. lose **b.** owner **c.** have **d.** carry

B. Read the following statements about the text and circle T (true) or F (false).

1. Fintech is a newly invented word.   (T / F)

2. Fintech is used to provide various financial services and products for
   businesses only.   (T / F)

3. Fintech has made it possible for aspiring entrepreneurs to obtain
   a loan from the bank.   (T / F)

4. In Japan, 2.9% of the population uses electronic money cards.   (T / F)

5. Presently, the majority of Japanese people prefer cash to electronic
   money.   (T / F)

C. Listen to the dialogue and fill in the missing words. 〔 59 〕

> **A:** I'm thinking of opening a nail salon, but I ₁. _____ _____
>
> _____ _____ a credit card terminal.
>
> **B:** I suggest you use a mobile credit card reader. It's a ₂. _____
>
> _____ _____ _____ to a smartphone or tablet,
>
> and it can read and process credit card payments.
>
> **A:** Sounds good. I ₃. _____ _____ _____
>
> _____ installing a terminal.
>
> **B:** It sure is. In fact, it's ₄. _____ _____ _____
>
> _____ like yours. You can even use it to accept payments outside of
>
> your store.

D. Below is the summary of the text. Rearrange the words inside the parentheses in the correct order. 〔 60 〕

Fintech is an abbreviation of the phrase "financial technology." Fintech has ₁. (us / of / finance / enabled / link / the / world / to) with IT, and it has created new financial services and products. In the business world, a ₂. (is / called / fintech-generated / used / entrepreneurs / system / crowdfunding / by) to raise capital over the Internet. In Japan the fintech industry is growing steadily, ₃. (to / still / people / but / prefer / cash) electronic money cards.

1. _____

2. _____

3. _____

Discussion

Do you think electronic money should replace cash as the main medium of exchange in Japan? What are the obstacles?

経済・ビジネス専門用語解説
Economic Terms and Topics

Unit 1　Inbound Tourism

Economic Terms

1　LCC（low-cost carrier ローコストキャリア）

　かつては，世界のどこでも，航空業界では，政府の規制等により航空運賃が一律に定められ，新規企業の参入が制限されていました。航空業界は，巨額の設備投資が必要であり新規参入が困難で，競争原理が働かず自然独占という市場の失敗が生じやすいため政府の規制が必要と考えられていました。国際線では IATA（国際航空運送協会）がカルテルを形成し価格決定権を有していました。しかしその後，「コンテスタビリティ理論」により規制緩和が行われました。1971 年のサウスウェスト航空が LCC の始まりで，価格自由化により 1 円航空券も登場するようになりました。

2　民泊

　民泊（みんぱく）とは，旅行者が一般の民家に宿泊することを指します。これまでは「宿泊料を受けて人を宿泊させる営業」をする場合には「旅館業法」に基づく営業許可の取得が必要でした。個人宅の空き部屋に旅行者を泊める「民泊」を推進し，規制緩和を行う必要があるということで，「住宅宿泊事業法」が 2018 年 6 月 15 日から施行されています。1 年間で貸し出す日数が 180 日を超えない場合には，旅館業法に基づく営業許可は不要です。

Topic　ホスピタリティ・インダストリー

　旅行業・観光業（ツーリズム）や，ホテル業などを総称する専門用語として，ホスピタリティ・インダストリーやホスピタリティ・ビジネスという用語があります。ホスピタリティ・インダストリーを「接客業」と翻訳することもあります。

　ホスピタリティ産業には，まず第一に，レストランやバー，クラブやカフェ，コーヒーショップ，ケータリングのように，顧客に食べ物や飲み物を提供する産業が含まれます。第二に，ホテルや旅館のように人に宿泊場所を提供するビジネスがあります。第三に，日本の JTB（Japan Travel Bureau）や HIS などに代表されるような旅行代理店（travel agency）や航空業界・鉄道業界などの運輸業界が含まれます。第四に，イベントプランナーの仕事や，カジノ，クルーズ船やテーマパークなども含まれます。

Unit **2** **Corporate Social Responsibility**

Economic Terms

1 ステークホルダー（利害関係者）

　英語の stakeholder は，そのまま「ステークホルダー」または「利害関係者」と訳されます。株式会社であれば，その代表的なステークホルダーは，その会社の株式を購入・投資している株主（shareholder）であり，それ以外に，その会社に融資している銀行やその株式会社の社債を購入している債権者（creditor），その会社の従業員（employee），取引先，顧客，地域社会・地元の住民などが利害関係者です。

2 コーポレート・ガバナンス（corporate governance 企業統治）

　コーポレート・ガバナンスとは，株主等を中心としたステークホルダーが，どのように企業の活動をコントロールし監視していくのかという仕組みのことをいいます。企業は社会的経済的影響力が大きく，独裁的な代表取締役社長が暴走すると，不祥事が生じたり株主の利益を害したり経済成長を阻害するといったことが生じてしまいます。日本の株価の低迷や経済の低迷の一因は，株主の力が弱い等のガバナンスの不在であると指摘する海外投資家が多く，日本では社外取締役の導入等の「ガバナンス改革」が進められています。

Topic　Sustainable Development Goals（SDGs）

　Sustainable Development Goals とは，一般的には，「持続可能な開発目標」と訳されます。どう発音するかというと，SDGs（エス・ディー・ジーズ）と読みます。SDGsは 2001 年に策定された「ミレニアム開発目標」を継ぐものであり，2015 年 9 月の国連サミットで採択された「持続可能な開発のための 2030 アジェンダ」に明記されており，国連加盟 193 か国が 2016 年から 2030 年の 15 年間で達成するために掲げた目標のことです。17 のゴールと 169 のターゲットから構成されており, 発展途上国を含めて「誰一人取り残さない（leave no one behind）」ことを誓っています。

　17 の目標は，「貧困をなくそう」，「飢餓をゼロに」，「すべての人に健康と福祉を」，「質の高い教育をみんなに」，「ジェンダー平等を実現しよう」，「安全な水とトイレを世界中に」，「エネルギーをみんなに　そしてクリーンに」，「働きがいも経済成長も」，「産業と技術革新の基盤をつくろう」，「人や国の不平等をなくそう」，「住み続けられるまちづくりを」，「つくる責任　つかう責任」，「気候変動に具体的な対策を」，「海の豊かさを守ろう」，「陸の豊かさも守ろう」，「平和と公正をすべての人に」，「パートナーシップで目標を達成しよう」です。

Unit 3　Aging Society

Economic Terms

1　介護保険制度（Long-Term Care Insurance System）

　公的介護保険制度は，1995 年にドイツで始まり，日本では 2000 年から実施されています。介護サービスを利用する場合には，費用の一定割合を利用者は負担しなければなりません。この負担割合は 1 割でしたが，2015 年 8 月から一定の所得のある方は 2 割を負担しなければならなくなりました。さらに 2018 年 8 月からは，現役並みの所得がある方は 3 割負担となり，合計所得金額により 1 割負担，2 割負担，3 割負担と負担割合が異なっています。

2　外国人看護師・外国人介護士（foreign care workers）

　日・インドネシア経済連携協定（EPA）に基づき 2008 年から，日・フィリピン経済連携協定に基づき 2009 年から，日・ベトナム経済連携協定に基づき 2014 年から，外国人看護師・介護福祉士候補者の受け入れを実施しています。累計での受入人数は 3 国併せて 6,400 人を超えていますが，言葉の壁は厚く，国家試験の合格率が低く，定着が進んでいません。

Topic　高齢化と少子化

　2017 年 4 月に，国立社会保障・人口問題研究所が発表した「日本の将来推計人口」における出生中位・死亡中位推計結果によると，65 歳以上人口は，「団塊の世代」が 75 歳以上となる 2025 年には 3,677 万人に達すると推計されています。その後も 65 歳以上人口は増加傾向にあり，2042 年に 3,935 万人でピークを迎えると予想しています。日本の高齢化率は直近では 28.4％ですが，2036 年に 33.3％に達し，3 人に 1 人が高齢者となる見込みです。2042 年以降は 65 歳以上人口が減少に転じても高齢化率は上昇を続け，2065 年には 38.4％に達すると推計しています。

　さらに深刻なのは少子化です。2020 年の出生数は 84 万人程度，2021 年の出生数は 80 万人程度と予想されています。コロナ禍で中国，米国，ヨーロッパなどでも世界的に少子化が加速しています。今後，日本の年金制度や社会保障制度はどうなってしまうのでしょうか。また世界はどうなっていくのでしょうか。

Unit 4　Empowerment of Women

Economic Terms

1　女性の職業生活における活躍の推進に関する法律
（Act on Promotion of Women's Participation and Advancement in the Workplace）

　「女性の職業生活における活躍の推進に関する法律」は，「女性活躍推進法」とも呼ばれます。職場で活躍したいという希望を持つすべての女性が，個性と能力を十分に発揮できる社会を実現するために，女性の活躍推進に向けた数値目標を盛り込んだ行動計画の策定・公表が国や地方公共団体，民間企業等に義務づけられています。従来は対象となる民間企業等は常用労働者 301 人以上でしたが，2022 年 4 月 1 日以降は 101 人以上に拡大されます。

2　男女共同参画社会基本法（Basic Law for a Gender-Equal Society）

　男女平等を推進するための法律である「男女共同参画社会基本法」は 1999 年から施行されています。日本においては，憲法に個人の尊重と法の下の平等がうたわれ，男女平等の実現に向けた様々な取り組みが着実に進められてきましたが，男女共同参画社会の実現に向けてなお一層の努力が必要とされており，この法律が制定されました。

Topic　　エンパワーメントとは

　「エンパワーメント」という概念はあいまいで多義的ですが，文字通りには，個人や集団が，発展・改革・成長に必要な力をつける，その能力を最大限発揮させるという意味の言葉です。ビジネスやジェンダーだけでなく，国際援助，ソーシャルワーク，まちづくりなどの分野でも用いられる専門用語です。ジェンダーの分野であれば，一般的には，女性が，力をつけ，能力を発揮し，かつ連帯して行動することによって，自分たちの置かれている不利な状況を変えていくという意味で使われます。

　また，経営学の分野では，「権限の委譲」という意味で使われることがあります。つまり現場に権限を与え，従業員の自主的・自律的な行動を引き出す支援活動という意味で「エンパワーメント」という用語が使われることがあります。

Unit 5   Consumption Tax

Economic Terms

1   OECD

　米国による戦後のヨーロッパ復興策であるマーシャル・プランの受入体制づくりのため，1948 年に欧州経済協力機構（OEEC）がパリに設立されました。その後，OEEC は改組され，1961 年に経済協力開発機構（Organisation for Economic Co-operation and Development）が設立されました。日本は 1964 年に加盟しました。OECD 加盟国の多くは先進国であるため，「OECD 加盟国の平均」は「先進国の平均」の意味で用いられることが多いといえます。

2   直接税（direct tax）と間接税（indirect tax）

　税を納める人（納税義務者）と負担する人（担税者）が同じ税金を「直接税（direct tax）」といい，税を納める人と負担する人が異なるものを「間接税（indirect tax）」といいます。たとえば，消費税や酒税やたばこ税は，商品などを購入した消費者が税を負担し，事業者が消費税を納めるため，間接税に分類されます。消費税の場合，メーカーや卸売業者や，スーパーなどの小売業者が，確定申告して消費税を納税します。

Topic   消費税の今後

　政府は，国防や警察や道路などの公共財を供給するサービスをしたり，社会保障として年金や医療費などを給付したり，教育などのサービスを提供します。そのために必要な資金を調達する方法としては，国債などの債券を発行する方法と，税を課す方法があります。何に対して税を課すかに着目して，租税は，所得課税と消費課税と資産課税に分類されます。

　日本では，2019 年 10 月に地方消費税を含めた消費税率を 10%に引き上げたことで，消費が落ち込み，2019 年 10 〜 12 月期の実質 GDP 成長率は年率換算で 7.1％も落ち込んでしまいました。こうした状況では消費税率を引き上げると景気が落ち込みかえって税収が減ってしまうこともありうるといえます。しかし国際通貨基金（IMF）は 2019 年 11 月に医療や介護などで増える社会保障費を賄うために，日本は 2030 年までに消費税率を 15% に上げる必要があると提言しました。

Unit **6**　**Deregulation**

Economic Terms

1　総合規制改革会議（Council for Promoting Regulatory Reform）

　総合規制改革会議は，規制改革を推進するために内閣府に設置され，2001 年 4 月 1 日から 2004 年 3 月 31 日に開催されましたが，2004 年度末をもって廃止されました。その後，担当する組織・会議の名称は何度も変わり，2019 年 10 月以降は，「規制改革推進会議」が規制改革について議論をおこなっています。

2　利益団体（interest group）

　特定の集団の利益を守り増進させるために社会や政府に働きかける団体のことを「利益団体」といいます。政治献金や投票行動に物をいわせて政治家に圧力をかけることから「圧力団体（pressure group）」と呼ばれることもあります。日本の例でいえば，経団連（日本経済団体連合会）・経済同友会・日本商工会議所（日商）などの経営者団体，連合などの労働団体，農協，日本医師会などが主要な利益団体です。

Topic　　正規社員の解雇規制緩和

　2013 年以降の第二次安倍内閣では，経済財政諮問会議，産業競争力会議，規制改革会議のそれぞれにおいて，解雇規制の緩和と労働市場の流動化が提言されています。

　日本では，正規社員の整理解雇に関する規制が非正規社員に比べて厳しすぎるために，日本の労働市場では，正規と非正規の二重構造が生じ，労働市場に歪みが生じてしまっているという議論がなされています。正規社員の解雇が難しいため，景気が冷え込むと企業が新卒の採用に極端に慎重になるため，これが「氷河期世代」を生み出し，少子化など様々な社会問題を生じさせたというのです。そこで，ある一定額の基本給を支払うことで解雇が可能となるといった「金銭解雇ルール」などが提案されています。

Unit 7   Official Development Assistance

Economic Terms

1　独立行政法人国際協力機構（Japan International Cooperation Agency）

　JICA は「ジャイカ」と読みます。外務省所管の独立行政法人であり，ODA（政府開発援助）の実施機関となっています。JICA のミッション（使命）は，開発協力大綱に基づいて，「人間の安全保障（human security）」と「質の高い成長」であるとされています。人間の安全保障とは，人間一人ひとりに着目して，保護と能力強化を通じ，持続可能な個人の自立と社会づくりを促そうという考え方のことをいいます。

2　財政赤字（fiscal deficit）

　日本の 2022 年度の一般会計予算では歳出が約 108 兆円で，税収が約 65 兆円しかないため，新規国債発行額は約 37 兆円となっています。

　国債と借入金，政府短期証券を合計した国の借金の残高は，2021 年 12 月末時点で 1,218 兆 4,330 億円と GDP の 2 倍を超えており，この比率は世界最悪と言ってよい状態にあります。さらに 2021 年度末 (2022 年 3 月 31 日) にはさらに約 86 兆円増え，約 1,304 兆円になる見込みです。

Topic　世界から貧困をなくすには

　経済を発展させるあるいは貧困をなくすためにはどうしたらよいのでしょうか。アダム・スミス的な考え方であれば，政府の市場への介入をできるだけなくし自由競争に委ねればよいでしょう。マルクスの考え方であれば，労働者が団結して社会主義革命を起こせばよいということになります。ジェフリー・サックスは発展途上国の陥っている貧困の罠を断ち切るには巨額の援助資金の投入，ビッグプッシュが必要と主張しました。これに対して，ウィリアム・イースタリーはアフリカに約 62 兆円も援助したにもかかわらず貧困からの脱却も経済成長もなかったと主張しました。これを「サックス vs イースタリー論争」といいます。

　2019 年のノーベル経済学賞は，アビジッド・バナジー，エステール・デュフロ，マイケル・クレマーの 3 人が貧困問題の実践的解決について受賞しました。医薬品開発などに用いられるランダム化比較試験（RCT）という手法を用いて，フィールド実験を行って途上国の抱える具体的問題と解決法について丹念に実証的に分析したことに対して賞が贈られました。経済学の学問の主流が，理論中心から実証研究中心となっている流れを反映しているといえます。

Unit 8　Microeconomics

Economic Terms

1　ミクロ経済学（microeconomics）

　ミクロ経済学では３つの経済主体（economic unit）が登場します。それが，企業（corporation）であり，家計（household）であり，政府（government）です。企業のことを「生産者（producer）」ともいいます。家計のことを「消費者（consumer）」ともいいます。家計は予算制約（budget constraint）のもとで，効用（utility）を最大化するように行動すると仮定されます。ここから需要曲線が導出されます。また企業は，利潤（profit）を最大にするように行動すると仮定され，ここから供給曲線が導出されます。

2　需要関数（demand function），供給関数（supply function）

　高校までの数学では $y = x + 5$ のような $y = f(x)$ という関数を学習します。ここで x のことを「独立変数（independent variable）」といい，y のことを「従属変数（dependent variable）」といいます。横軸が独立変数で縦軸が従属変数なわけです。しかし需要関数とは $D = -P + 10$ のような関数を指すので，従属変数と独立変数の関係が，高校までの縦軸・横軸の関係と逆になるのです。一般に需要曲線は右下がりとなりますが，これを「需要法則」といいます。

Topic　　需要曲線と供給曲線とそれらのシフト

　ミクロ経済学の基本となる需要と供給の関係は理解しにくいものです。「価格が下がると需要が増える」ことと「需要が増えると価格が上昇する」という両方の関係を説明できますか。需要法則を意味する「価格が下がると需要（量）が増える」という関係は，静止した需要曲線上の２点間の移動として説明されます。他方で，「需要が増えると価格が上昇する」というのは，需要曲線が右（上）にシフトして，均衡価格が上昇するという意味です。

　Reading の文章では生産費用や租税政策の変化によって供給曲線がシフトすると述べられていますが，厳密には限界費用（marginal cost）の上昇や従量税・従価税の賦課によって，供給曲線は左上方にシフトします。他方で，企業が技術進歩などで生産性を上げ限界費用の削減を実現していくと供給曲線は右下方にシフトします。財（goods）には上級財（superior goods）と下級財（inferior goods）があり，家計所得が増えた場合に需要が増えるのは上級財であるため，上級財の場合には家計所得が増えると需要曲線が右上にシフトします。

Unit 9　Macroeconomics

Economic Terms

1　米ドル（USD）

アメリカの法定通貨は「ドル」ですが，「ドル」という名前の通貨が他の国にもあるため，アメリカのドルのことを他と区別するときには「米ドル」などといいます。米ドル以外に，カナダ・ドル，オーストラリア・ドル，ニュージーランド・ドル，香港・ドル，シンガポール・ドルなどがあり，これらは米ドルと違う，すべて別の異なる通貨です。

2　設備投資（business investment）

投資という言葉を聞くと，株式投資や債券投資といった証券投資を思い浮かべると思います。しかし経済学（マクロ経済学）では株式投資などの証券投資は投資ではありません。「投資（investment）」とは，民間企業の設備投資，在庫投資（inventory investment），住宅投資（housing investment）のことをいいます。そして，「設備投資」とは，企業が，生産能力の拡大，現有設備の老朽化に伴う更新や合理化などのために，あるいは将来の収益を期待して，建物や生産設備を購入することをいいます。

Topic　ジョン・メイナード・ケインズとアルフレッド・マーシャル

アルフレッド・マーシャルの考え方によると，失業が起こったとしてもそれは一時的なものであると考えます。賃金（実質賃金）が高すぎると，多くの労働者が働きたいと思い（労働供給が多い），他方で企業はあまり人を雇わないので（労働需要は少ない），労働供給＞労働需要となり，失業が発生します。しかし市場メカニズムにより，賃金が下落するので，労働需要＝労働供給という均衡状態が実現し，失業のない状態，完全雇用が実現されると考えます。ところが 1929 年からアメリカでは 4 人に 1 人が失業者という世界大恐慌が起こります。ケインズは，失業の発生により賃金が下落すると所得が減り，消費が減り GDP が減ってしまい，これがさらに消費を減少させ，ますます GDP を減少させてしまうといってマーシャルを批判したのです。そして失業対策，政府による財政政策や金融政策などの景気対策の必要性をケインズは説いたのです。ケインズ的経済政策には多くの批判があるのですが，リーマンショックやコロナショックの際にはケインズ的な景気政策が発動されています。

Unit 10 Balance of Payments

Economic Terms

1 国際収支（Balance of Payments，略して BP）

　国際収支統計の用語は頻繁に変更されているので注意が必要です。現在でも国際収支は経常収支と資本収支から構成されているという旧統計の解説はよく見かけますが，2014 年から IMF「国際収支マニュアル第 6 版」が適用されており，現在の国際収支統計では，「国際収支＝経常収支＋資本移転等収支－金融収支＋誤差脱漏＝0」であり，国際収支の二本柱は，「経常収支」と「金融収支」です。第 5 版では，「BP＝経常収支＋資本収支＋外貨準備増減＋誤差脱漏＝0」でしたので，国際収支の柱は経常収支と資本収支でした。

2 経常収支（current account，略して CA）

　経常収支の項目についても用語が頻繁に変更されています。IMF「国際収支マニュアル第 5 版」では，「経常収支＝貿易・サービス収支＋所得収支（payment of interest and dividends）＋経常移転収支（foreign aid transfers）」ですが，第 6 版の用語では，所得収支の代わりに「第一次所得収支」，経常移転収支の代わりに「第二次所得収支」という用語をもちいますので，「経常収支＝貿易・サービス収支＋第一次所得収支＋第二次所得収支」となっています。

Topic　　日本の経常収支と対外純資産

　2020 年の日本の国際収支統計の数字を見てみると，貿易収支は 3 兆 457 億円の黒字となっています。2020 年はコロナ禍により訪日外国人が減少したため，旅行収支は約 5,621 億円の黒字にとどまりました。2019 年は約 2 兆 7,023 億円の黒字でした。利子（interest）や配当（dividends）などの投資収益の海外とのやりとりを示す第 1 次所得収支は 20 兆 7,175 億円の巨額の黒字です。第 2 次所得収支は約 2.5 兆円の赤字です。合計して経常収支は約 18 兆円の黒字です。このおかげで，巨額の財政赤字や国の借金があっても比較的円が強く，経済が豊かな状態を維持することができているのです。経常収支黒字が長年続いたため，日本の企業や政府や個人が海外に持つ資産から負債を引いた対外純資産残高は 2019 年末時点で 364 兆 5,250 億円となっており，日本は世界最大の純債権国（対外純資産国）です。日本は輸出で食べているというより海外投資で食べている国なわけです。

Unit 11   Strong Yen/Weak Yen

Economic Terms

1　固定為替相場制（fixed exchange rate system）と変動為替相場制（floating exchange rate system）

　第二次世界大戦が終わり，戦後の国際通貨体制のブレトン・ウッズ体制の下では，金ドル本位制に基づく固定為替相場制が採用され，金1オンス＝35ドル，1ドル＝360円でした。またイギリスの通貨ポンドとの関係では，1949年から1967年までは1ポンド＝1,008円でした。1973年以降変動為替相場制に移行し，2021年4月現在では，1ドル＝110円付近，1ポンド＝150円付近ですが，今後どうなるのでしょう。

2　貿易黒字国（trade surplus country）

　日本の貿易収支は，戦後当初は赤字で，1960年代後半には黒字になりはじめましたが，1973年と79年の石油危機では一時的な赤字を経験しました。日本で貿易黒字額が過去最高となったのは1992年で，約16兆円の黒字となりました。東日本大震災の後，日本は貿易赤字に転じ，2011年から2015年まで貿易赤字でした。国際収支統計では最近は日本の貿易収支は黒字ですが黒字額はわずかです。他方で，アメリカでは2020年は貿易赤字の額は約100兆円，2020年度の財政赤字の額は約330兆円でした。アメリカの対外純負債は1,000兆円を超えます。

Topic　　為替レートの決定要因

　変動相場制の下では，為替レートは需要と供給によって決まるわけですが，それ以外にも，物価水準（インフレ率）や金利や金融政策の動向，経常収支，失業率や経済成長率などの景気動向や市場心理（期待・予想）によっても変動します。一般に物価上昇率が高い国の通貨は，その通貨の価値が下がることにつながるため売られやすくなります。一般に，金利の低い国の通貨は売られやすく，金利の高い国の通貨は買われるため，FRB（連邦準備制度理事会）が利下げを決めると一般的にドルを売って円を買う動きが進むことが多いです。

　アメリカの経済のファンダメンタルズを見た場合，アメリカは1,000兆円を超える巨額の債務国であり，貿易赤字，経常赤字や財政赤字も巨額であるため，米ドルは暴落してもおかしくないはずです。アメリカは国際政治のリーダーであり，軍事力があり，長い間，貿易決済などで米ドルが使われ続けたために，米ドルが基軸通貨のままなのです。日本は北朝鮮やロシアや中国に囲まれ地政学的に不利であり，敗戦国であり，円の国際化は失敗したといわれます。中国は経済大国ですが，共産党独裁の政治体制は信用されておらず，国際決済に人民元が使われる割合はまだ2%程度です。

Unit 12　Mergers and Acquisitions (M&A)

Economic Terms

1　本業による自律的成長（organic growth）

「自律的成長」とは，企業内部に蓄積された商品やサービス，技術などの，既存の事業・資源をいかして自律的に収益を拡大させていくことを意味します。反対概念は，企業の合併や買収（M&A）によって新規事業や新製品を外部から取り込み収益を伸ばすという意味の M&A グロースで，このことを「non organic growth」ともいいます。

2　TOB（takeover bid 株式公開買い付け）

上場企業を買収するとき，東京証券取引所（東証）などで大量に株を買い占めて 50% 超を買えば乗っ取りができます。ただし株価が上昇し買収資金がかかりすぎてしまうときがあり，この場合 TOB を使います。2019 年に伊藤忠商事はデサントに TOB をかけたのですが，デサントの株主に対し，東証の株価の 1 株 1,871 円に対し，1 株 2,800 円で買うから株を伊藤忠に売るように呼びかけました。日本で数少ない敵対的 TOB の成功例です。

Topic　日本企業と M&A

かつて，日本では M&A には悪いイメージがありました。グリーンメーラーといって，上場企業の株式を買い占め，買い占めた株を会社や役員などに高値で買い取らせようという投資家がいました。また，堀江貴文社長のライブドアによるニッポン放送株の買い占めや，村上世彰が率いる村上ファンドによる東京スタイル株の買い占めがあり，バブル崩壊後の外資系ファンド，つまりハゲタカファンドの行動に批判が集まり，敵対的 M&A に対しては悪いイメージが完全に定着してしまいました。しかし株式会社を上場すれば，だれでも株が買えるわけで，法律を守っている限り，買い占めを批判することはできないはずです。

近年では，欧米では完全に定着した M&A を経営戦略に生かそうという企業が着実に増えています。今後, 日本では中小企業が当事者となる M&A と, クロスボーダー M&A（外国企業による日本企業の買収，日本企業による外国企業の買収）がますます増えていくと予想されています。2019 年には, 武田薬品工業が, アイルランドの製薬大手のシャイアーを約 6 兆 2000 億円の買収金額で買収しました。

Unit 13 Individual Investors

Economic Terms

1 NISA（少額投資非課税制度）

NISA は，2014 年 1 月に始まった個人投資家のための税制優遇制度です。NISA では，毎年 120 万円の非課税投資枠が設定され，株式・株式投資信託の配当や収益分配金や譲渡益が非課税の対象となっています。これは，イギリスの ISA（Individual Savings Account　個人貯蓄口座）をモデルとしており，NISA（ニーサ　Nippon Individual Savings Account）という愛称がついています。2020 年現在，通常の NISA，未成年者向けのジュニア NISA，つみたて NISA の 3 種類があります。

2 普通預金口座（savings account）

銀行の預金口座には小切手の決済に使う checking account（当座預金）と savings account（普通預金）があります。しかし savings account という用語は厳密には利子がつく口座という意味です。checking account は主にアメリカ英語で，イギリスでは current account という用語があり，これも小切手決済用なので「当座預金」と訳してもよいのですが，日本の普通預金に近いので「普通預金」と訳すときもあります。current account には原則的に利子がつきません。日本の定期預金を的確に表現するためには time deposit，term deposit という用語があります。

Topic　日本の個人投資家

株式投資にはリスクが伴い，その会社が倒産すると，株価が 0 円になる，つまり株式が紙くずになる可能性があるため，お金持ちでなければ株式投資はできません。

第二次世界大戦前の日本は，格差社会で，地主や超富裕層や財閥家族といったお金持ちがいたため，1945 年度末の時点では過半数の株式が個人投資家によって所有されていたのです。ところが空襲や戦後のインフレや農地改革や財閥解体や公職追放により，お金持ちが没落してしまったのです。財閥解体によって財閥本社が放出した株式を買い取ったのは，個人投資家ではなくてメインバンクや取引先などの系列企業でした。会社が株式を所有するという法人資本主義の時代となり，1957 年度末の法人持株比率は 72% に達し，個人投資家は完全に少数派になりました。「一億総中流」という平等な社会にはなりましたが，資本主義を支えるリスクマネーの供給者がいない社会になってしまいました。

しかし時代は変化しつつあります。日本も格差社会となり，証券取引所の株式分布状況調査では個人株主数の増加が続いています。東京証券取引所の投資主体別売買代金比率をみると 6 割から 7 割が外国人投資家で約 2 割が個人投資家で，法人の売買は少ないのです。

Unit 14　Big Data

Economic Terms

1　人工知能（artificial intelligence）

人工知能の定義は論者により異なりますが，アルゴリズムとデータに基づき判断を行って人の頭脳活動などを代替する技術であるといえます。ディープラーニング（深層学習）の技術の進展とビッグデータの普及により，第三次 AI ブームが起きています。ただし現状で AI ができるのは，ほぼ「音声認識」と「自然言語処理」と「画像解析」に限られています。

2　戦略（strategy）とオペレーション（operation）とマネジメント（management）

ビジネスや IT の世界では，英語をもとにしたカタカナ言葉が非常に多く用いられます。変化が速く日本語の訳語がまだなかったり，訳語が定着しないといったことが起きているからです。経営戦略のことを「ストラテジー」といいます。日常業務を運営する手順を定めること，その手順に沿って実施する一連の作業を「オペレーション」といいます。「マネジメント」とはヒト・モノ・カネ・情報などを管理することです。

Topic　　ビッグデータ

ビッグデータの特徴として 3V が挙げられることがよくあります。これは high-volume（データの量の多さ），high-velocity（更新頻度），high-variety（データ種類の多様性）の 3 つを指します。

自動車産業におけるビッグデータの活用事例として「テレマティクス」があります。テレマティクスでは自動車にスマートフォンやカーナビを接続し，渋滞情報や位置情報や天気予報などの情報サービスを提供しています。

飲料メーカーのダイドードリンコは，自動販売機をみたときの顧客の視線のデータを収集し，主力商品を自動販売機のどこにおくかを決めています。

残念ながら，スイスの有力ビジネススクール IMD による 2019 年の「世界競争力ランキング」によると，ビッグデータの活用・分析について，日本は最下位になっています。

Unit 15　Fintech

Economic Terms

1　仮想通貨（virtual currency）

　仮想通貨は，日本円や米ドルのような法定通貨とは異なり，「特定の国による価値の保証のない通貨」であって，「暗号化されたデジタル通貨」です。crypto-asset という語もよくつかわれており，日本の金融商品取引法や資金決済法などでは，「暗号資産」という用語を用いています。ビットコインなど「仮想通貨」「暗号資産」には，600 種類以上の通貨があります。

2　クラウドファンディング（crowdfunding）

　クラウドファンディングとは，「群衆（crowd）」と「資金調達（funding）」をつなぎあわせた語で，インターネットをとおして不特定多数の人々から資金を調達することを指します。プロジェクトに寄付するだけで見返りがない「寄付型」，資金提供の見返りとして商品やサービスを購入する「購入型」，お金を貸す「融資型」・「貸付型」，出資する「投資型」などがあります。

Topic　デジタル・トランスフォーメーション（DX）

　フィンテック技術は，既存の金融機関のビジネスにとって脅威になっているわけですが，金融に限らず，IT 技術はこれまでのビジネスのあり方や人々の生活を大きく変えつつあります。2004 年にスウェーデンのエリック・ストルターマン教授が「デジタル・トランスフォーメーション（DX）」という用語を提唱しましたが，それがまさに起こりつつあるのです。
　例えばアマゾンは巨大な電子商取引のプラットフォームを構築し，ユーザーはどこにいても何でも好きなものが買えるようになりました。アマゾンはその後，AWS（Amazon Web Services）というクラウドサービスを提供するようになっています。またアメリカのGAFA（グーグル，アップル，フェイスブック（メタ），アマゾン）や中国の BAT（バイドゥ，アリババ，テンセント）といった巨大プラットフォーマーは決済を中心とした金融領域にも進出しています。これから IT は私たちの生活をどこまで変えてしまうのでしょうか。

著　者
Mark Chang（マーク　チャン）　　昭和女子大学
堀口　和久（ほりぐち　かずひさ）　　千葉経済大学

総合英語：日本の経済を知る・社会を見る

2023 年 2 月 20 日　第 1 版発行
2024 年 3 月 20 日　第 3 版発行

著　者——Mark Chang ／堀口和久
発行者——前田俊秀
発行所——株式会社　三修社
　　　　　〒 150-0001　東京都渋谷区神宮前 2-2-22
　　　　　TEL 03-3405-4511 / FAX 03-3405-4522
　　　　　振替 00190-9-72758
　　　　　https://www.sanshusha.co.jp
　　　　　編集担当　三井るり子・伊藤宏実

印刷所——広研印刷株式会社

表紙 デザイン—NONdesign
準拠音声制作—高速録音株式会社
準拠音声録音—ELEC（吹込：Josh Keller / Karen Haedrich）

教科書準拠 CD 発売
本書の準拠 CD をご希望の方は弊社までお問い合わせください。

ズバリ よくでる → 直前

チェック BOOK

漢字の読み書き・文法重要事項に完全対応!

国語

教育出版版

1年

赤 シートで 何度でも!

漢字の練習1
教 p.29

平仮名を書く。（ ひらがな ）
貴い身分。（ とうと ）
委員に推す。（ お ）
新商品を試す。（ ため ）
危うい状態。（ あや ）
人形を操る。（ あや ）
人々が集う。（ つど ）
秘めた思い。（ ひ ）
災いを防ぐ。（ わざわ ）
小銭ではらう。（ こぜに ）
花の園を歩く。（ その ）
幸多かれ。（ さち ）
情報に基づく。（ もと ）
神業に驚く。（ かみわざ ）
グラフの値。（ あたい ）
速やかに動く。（ すみ ）
蔵元の酒。（ くらもと ）
武道の技。（ わざ ）

胸苦しい感覚。（ むなぐる ）
一斉に言う。（ いっせい ）
バットを振る。（ ふ ）
絶海の孤島。（ ことう ）
耳鼻科に行く。（ じびか ）
一朝一夕。（ いっせき ）
暮春の風景。（ ぼしゅん ）

自分の脳を知っていますか
教 p.32〜40

奇妙な現象。（ みょう ）
話すときの癖。（ くせ ）
意見の比較。（ ひかく ）
姉の背を抜く。（ ぬ ）
混乱に陥る。（ おちい ）
互いに支える。（ たが ）

漢字の広場1
教 p.44〜45

違う考え方。（ ちが ）
侮辱した態度。（ ぶ ）

テストでまちがえやすい漢字

覚悟を決める。（ かくご ）
素朴な人柄。（ そぼく ）
雑草を刈る。（ か ）
顎ひげをそる。（ あご ）
窒素の性質。（ ちっそ ）
草木が茂る。（ しげ ）
充実した生活。（ じゅうじつ ）
金品を盗む。（ ぬす ）
過去の怨念。（ おんねん ）
天下泰平の世。（ たいへい ）
九分九厘。（ くりん ）
音痴を直す。（ おんち ）
扇であおぐ。（ おうぎ ）
刑務所の囚人。（ しゅうじん ）
恣意的な判断。（ しい ）
港湾の船。（ こうわん ）
妊娠中の女性。（ にんしん ）
安らかな睡眠。（ すいみん ）
寝室に入る。（ しんしつ ）

2

表彰状を渡す。（ひょうしょう）（わた）

頑固な性格。（がんこ）

免疫がある。（めんえき）

廃棄処分する。（はいき）

匿名のお便り。（とくめい）

数字の羅列。（られつ）

広い敷地。（しきち）

才媛の誉れ。（さいえん）（ほま）

ベンチ 教 p.52〜61

僕の意見。（ぼく）

我慢の限界。（がまん）

東京の郊外。（こうがい）

花の匂い。（におい）

爪先を伸ばす。（つまさき）

突然の来客。（とつぜん）

彼女の荷物。（かのじょ）

かばんを提げる。（さ）

網で虫をとる。（あみ）

紙でできた袋。（ふくろ）

遠くを眺める。（なが）

本が欲しい。（ほ）

岩の裂け目。（さ）

幼稚園に行く。（ようちえん）

田舎で暮らす。（いなか）

鍋に蓋をする。（なべ）（ふた）

物々交換をする。（こうかん）

玄関に上がる。（げんかん）

別れの挨拶。（あいさつ）

じっと黙る。（だま）

乳母車に乗せる。（うば）

ボタンを押す。（お）

無知を恥じる。（は）

腰を下ろす。（こし）

膝を曲げる。（ひざ）

雑誌に載る。（の）

恐ろしい話。（おそ）

道で転倒する。（てんとう）

休暇をとる。（きゅうか）

子どもを叱る。（しか）

漢字の広場2 教 p.68〜69

索引の利用。（さくいん）

知識の確認。（かくにん）

滋味に富む。（じみ）

興奮を抑える。（おさ）

犯人の逮捕。（たい）

巨大な陵墓。（りょうぼ）

小さな隙間。（すきま）

狩猟を禁じる。（しゅりょう）

神社に詣でる。（もう）

家畜を育てる。（かちく）

険しい崖。（がけ）

遺言を残す。（ゆいごん）

海亀の生態。（うみがめ）

鳥の産卵。（さんらん）

赤く熟れた果物。（う）

意見に納得する。（なっとく）

ズバッ 健やかに育つ。（すこ）

ズバッ 廊下を歩く。（ろうか）

部屋の掃除。（そうじ）

一周忌の法要。（いっしゅうき）

ズバッ 近郷に住む人々。（きんごう）

ズバッ 干潟を歩く。（ひがた）

ズバッ 瓶に水を入れる。（びん）

食卓につく。（しょくたく）

ズバッ 激しい葛藤。（かっとう）

京浜方面。（けいひん）

森には魔法つかいがいる　教 p.86〜97

ズバッ 魔法を唱える。（まほう）

入り江の生き物。（え）

ズバッ 泥水が流れる。（どろみず）

小さな粒子。（りゅうし）

ズバッ 壊滅的な状況。（かい）

漢字の練習2　教 p.107

部活の先輩。（せんぱい）

お金を費やす。（つい）

ズバッ 本棚を置く。（ほんだな）

危険を伴う。（ともな）

ズバッ 漫画を買う。（まんが）

謎を解く。（なぞ）

ズバッ 庶民の感覚。（しょみん）

虎がほえる。（とら）

交響楽の曲。（こうきょうがく）

頑丈な扉。（とびら）

ズバッ 普通のこと。（ふつう）

ズバッ 麦の穂がゆれる。（ほ）

ズバッ 報酬を支払う。（ほうしゅう）

大声で叫ぶ。（さけ）

状況を把握する。（あく）

準備に慌てる。（あわ）

ズバッ 小説の注釈。（ちゅうしゃく）

五月晴れ。（さつき）

ズバッ テストでまちがえやすい漢字

部屋を立ち退く。（たちのく）

大和言葉を学ぶ。（やまと）

物語の始まり ―竹取物語―　教 p.114〜121

殿様とお姫様。（ひめ）

子どもの頃。（ころ）

ズバッ 求婚する相手。（きゅうこん）

竜の落とし子。（たつ）

誰かを呼ぶ。（だれ）

ズバッ 客を迎える。（むか）

罪を犯す。（おか）

ズバッ きれいな羽衣。（はごろも）

手紙を渡す。（わた）

ズバッ 父が落胆する。（らくたん）

故事成語 ―中国の名言―　教 p.122〜126

矛盾した発言。（むじゅん）

反応が鋭い。（　するど　）

猿の飼育。（　さる　）

竜頭蛇尾。（　び　）

苗を植える。（　なえ　）

疲れをとる。（　つか　）

息子が生まれる。（　むすこ　）

花が枯れる。（　か　）

蜘蛛の糸 教 p.128〜137

極楽浄土。（　ごくらく　）

桜が咲く。（　さ　）

布で覆う。（　おお　）

天国と地獄。（　じごく　）

美しい水晶。（　すいしょう　）

透けて見える。（　す　）

一緒に遊ぶ。（　いっしょ　）

二匹の子ねこ。（　にひき　）

道端の雑草。（　みちばた　）

踏み台に乗る。（　ふ　）

報いを受ける。（　むく　）

水に浮く。（　う　）

船が沈む。（　しず　）

暗闇の中。（　くらやみ　）

懸命に働く。（　けんめい　）

中途で引き返す。（　ちゅうと　）

隠れた才能。（　かく　）

結果に驚く。（　おどろ　）

聞くに堪えない。（　た　）

肝腎要の部分。（　かんじん　）

無慈悲な対応。（　じひ　）

厳しい罰。（　ばつ　）

頓着しない。（　とんちゃく　）

漢字の練習3 教 p.138

韓国へ行く。（　かんこく　）

升目に合わせる。（　ますめ　）

屯田兵の歴史。（　とんでんへい　）

牛丼を作る。（　ぎゅうどん　）

猫を飼う。（　ねこ　）

亜熱帯の地域。（　あねったい　）

甚だしい損害。（　はなは　）

美しく変貌する。（　へんぼう　）

一つ又は二つ。（　また　）

賞状を授与する。（　じゅよ　）

霊長類の調査。（　れいちょうるい　）

平凡な生活。（　へいぼん　）

書斎にこもる。（　しょさい　）

焦点を当てる。（　しょうてん　）

問題を捉える。（　とら　）

五月雨が降る。（　さみだれ　）

三味線を習う。（　しゃみせん　）

梅雨が明ける。（　つゆ　）

日和をうかがう。（　ひより　）

河童と蛙 教 p.140〜145

ダンスを踊る。（　おど　）

底なしの沼。（　ぬま　）

嵐に備える。（あらし）

火山が噴火する。（ふんか）

農業が盛んだ。（さか）

丸太を縛る。（しば）

旅行の支度。（したく）

励ましの手紙。（はげ）

手紙を添える。（そ）

躍起になる。（やっき）

騒がしい声。（さわ）

優しい性格。（やさ）

年度が替わる。（か）

痩せた犬。（や）

威勢がいい。（いせい）

斜めにかたむく。（なな）

象の牙。（きば）

お金を稼ぐ。（かせ）

偉い人物。（えら）

鎖をつなぐ。（くさり）

靴をぬぐ。（くつ）

サンダルを履く。（は）

閉じ込める。（こ）

何杯もの水。（なんばい）

十把ひとからげ。（じっぱ）

愉快な話。（ゆかい）

薪を拾う。（たきぎ）

鍛冶職人になる。（かじ）

ソファに座る。（すわ）

星空を仰ぐ。（あお）

意気地がない。（いくじ）

早速取りかかる。（さっそく）

碁の対局を見る。（ご）

オツベルと象 教 p.146〜164

風呂が沸く。（わ）

長唄の鑑賞。（ながうた）

泡がたつ。（あわ）

稲を刈る。（いね）

腰を据える。（す）

百姓の仕事。（ひゃくしょう）

広大な砂漠。（さばく）

煙がたなびく。（けむり）

薄い冊子。（うす）

口笛を吹く。（ふ）

頑丈な造り。（がんじょう）

雑巾をしぼる。（ぞうきん）

国民の皆さん。（みな）

床を掃除する。（ゆか）

忙しい毎日。（いそが）

奥まで進む。（おく）

退屈な話。（たいくつ）

漢字の練習4 教 p.168

故人の追悼。（ついとう）

蚊が血を吸う。（か）

線香花火。（せんこう）

蚕の繭。（まゆ）

純粋な人。（じゅんすい）

翼を広げる。（つばさ）
紫外線を浴びる。（しがいせん）
太陽は恒星だ。（こうせい）
蜂蜜を食べる。（はちみつ）
陶器のつぼ。（とうき）
千羽鶴を送る。（せんばづる）
工夫をこらす。（くふう）
幽閉される。（ゆうへい）
理想には程遠い。（ほどとお）
門松を立てる。（かどまつ）
来る日曜日。（きた）
昆虫を飼う。（こんちゅう）
新作の披露。（ひろう）
畑の畝。（うね）
捻挫が治る。（ねんざ）

子どもの権利 教 p.170〜177
虐待に反対する。（ぎゃくたい）
機会を奪う。（うば）

中学生を含む。（ふく）

漢字の広場3 教 p.182〜183
菊の花が咲く。（きく）
峠の向こう。（とうげ）
蛇口をひねる。（じゃぐち）
歩幅が広い。（ほはば）
米の銘柄。（めい）
美しい小紋。（こもん）
映画の脇役。（わきやく）
杉の木の花粉。（すぎ）
部屋の片隅。（かたすみ）
童話の影絵。（かげえ）
小さな鈴の音。（すず）
松の盆栽。（ぼんさい）
養豚場を営む。（ようとん）
曇天の空模様。（どんてん）
曖昧な返答。（あいまい）
厄介な問題。（やっ）

倉庫の錠前。（じょうまえ）
雑煮を食べる。（ぞうに）
剣玉で遊ぶ。（けんだま）
茶釜のお湯。（ちゃがま）
激しい火炎。（かえん）
逃走する犯人。（とうそう）
滝に打たれる。（たき）
白髪の老翁。（ろうおう）
北斗七星。（ほくと）
静かな河畔。（かはん）
臼歯が生える。（きゅうし）
抑揚をつける。（よくよう）

漢字の練習5 教 p.185
柔軟な思考。（じゅうなん）
外科に通う。（げか）
発憤する。（はっぷん）
世紀の傑作。（けっさく）
生活の基盤。（きばん）

	言葉がつなぐ世界遺産 教p.200〜211	

必須の条件。（ひっす）

成分の分析。（ぶんせき）

果敢な試み。（かかん）

土砂が流れる。（どしゃ）

一切わからない。（いっさい）

清貧を旨とする。（せいひん）

大会の主催。（しゅさい）

時計を携帯する。（けいたい）

天然の城郭。（じょうかく）

痛恨のミス。（つうこん）

事業の大綱。（たいこう）

狭い部屋。（せま）

辛辣な意見。（しんらつ）

肥沃な土壌。（ひよく）

赤字の累積。（るいせき）

暴動の鎮静化。（ちんせい）

妥協案を出す。（だきょう）

某国の宰相。（さいしょう）

音沙汰がない。（さた）

詩の比喩表現。（ひゆ）

弦楽器を弾く。（げんがっき）

備忘録を書く。（びぼう）

日光の東照宮。（とうしょうぐう）

装飾を施す。（そうしょく）

豪華な客船。（ごうか）

三棟のビル。（さんとう）

お寺の境内。（けいだい）

窓を閉ざす。（と）

環境を整える。（かんきょう）

湿気を防ぐ。（しっけ）

氷の彫刻。（ちょうこく）

鮮やかな色。（あざ）

つやのある漆。（うるし）

剥落した樹皮。（はくらく）

審査の基準。（しんさ）

夢に描く。（えが）

迫力がある。（はくりょく）

微妙な判定。（びみょう）

丁寧な説明。（てい）

高い塔に登る。（とう）

軒下で休む。（のきした）

朱色の皿。（しゅいろ）

塩分が濃い。（こ）

澄んだ瞳。（ひとみ）

ペンキを塗る。（ぬ）

同級生を頼る。（たよ）

彩色にこだわる。（さいしき）

詳細に検討する。（しょうさい）

繊細な気持ち。（せんさい）

弟子に教える。（でし）

布の肌ざわり。（はだ）

師弟の関係。（してい）

知人宅を訪れる。（おとず）

8

9

漢字の広場4　教p.230〜231

- 雷鳴が響く。（らいめい）
- 名峰を訪ねる。（めいほう）
- 広大な砂丘。（さきゅう）
- 舞台に上がる。（ぶたい）
- 腕力が強い。（わんりょく）
- 野菜の出荷。（しゅっか）
- 企業の戦略。（きぎょう）
- 大きな拍手。（はくしゅ）
- 二つが並立する。（へいりつ）
- 洞窟に入る。（どうくつ）
- 人体の解剖。（かいぼう）
- 壮大な計画。（そうだい）
- 誤字の訂正。（ていせい）
- 険しい山岳。（さんがく）
- 是非を問う。（ぜひ）
- 感性の鈍化。（どんか）
- 禍福を占う。（かふく）
- 漏水を防ぐ。（ろうすい）

- 文を添削する。（てんさく）
- 剛性が高い。（ごうせい）
- 憂鬱な空模様。（ゆううつ）
- 遷都の歴史。（せんと）
- 油脂の採取。（ゆし）
- 秀麗な富士山。（しゅうれい）
- 不朽の名作。（ふきゅう）
- 犬の嗅覚。（きゅうかく）
- 美しい環礁。（かんしょう）
- 仲の良い姉妹。（しまい）

漢字の練習6　教p.233

- 道路が渋滞する。（じゅうたい）
- 柿を食べる。（かき）
- 桃を買う。（もも）
- 邦楽と洋楽。（ほうがく）
- 海藻のサラダ。（かいそう）
- きれいな河川。（かせん）
- 適切な措置。（そち）

- 計画の進捗。（しんちょく）
- 軽い症状。（しょうじょう）
- 種痘を施す。（しゅとう）
- 下痢を起こす。（げり）
- 利潤の追求。（りじゅん）
- 床が浸水する。（しんすい）
- 唾液の分泌。（ぶんぴつ）
- 土地の坪数。（つぼすう）
- 貝塚の発見。（かいづか）
- 大規模な古墳。（こふん）
- 豊かな土壌。（どじょう）
- 生活の困窮。（こんきゅう）
- 窃盗の被害。（せっとう）
- 備前焼の窯元。（かまもと）
- 邸宅を構える。（ていたく）
- 桑畑が広がる。（くわばたけ）
- 新郎と新婦。（しんろう）
- 皇帝の外叔。（がいしゅく）

少年の日の思い出

教 p.240〜256

やすりで擦る。（　す　）

珍しい昆虫。（　めずら　）

微笑をもらす。（　びしょう　）

遊戯にふける。（　ゆうぎ　）

胴乱を提げる。（　どうらん　）

惰眠を貪る。（　むさぼ　）

忍び寄る影。（　しの　）

まだらの斑点。（　はんてん　）

虫の触角。（　しょっかく　）

歓喜の表情。（　かんき　）

耳栓をする。（　みみせん　）

シールを貼る。（　は　）

果物が傷む。（　いた　）

模範的な態度。（　もはん　）

相手を妬む。（　ねた　）

絵画の鑑定。（　かんてい　）

本の挿絵。（　さしえ　）

熱烈な応援。（　ねつれつ　）

幾度もの失敗。（　いくど　）

布団を畳む。（　たた　）

出世を羨む。（　うらや　）

優雅な生活。（　ゆうが　）

誘惑に負ける。（　ゆう　）

丹念に調べる。（　たんねん　）

依然雨が続く。（　いぜん　）

軽蔑に値する。（　けいべつ　）

丁重に扱う。（　あつか　）

喉笛が鳴る。（　のどぶえ　）

激しく罵る。（　ののし　）

罪を償う。（　つぐな　）

返事が遅い。（　おそ　）

漢字の練習7

教 p.258

柳の下に立つ。（　やなぎ　）

戒めを守る。（　いまし　）

小説の抄録。（　しょうろく　）

患者の世話。（　かんじゃ　）

テストでまちがえやすい漢字

前言撤回する。（　てっかい　）

哺乳類の一種。（　ほにゅうるい　）

王に謁見する。（　えっけん　）

獣医になりたい。（　じゅうい　）

澄んだ川の流れ。（　す　）

試合に惜敗する。（　せきはい　）

小豆を煮る。（　あずき　）

海原が広がる。（　うなばら　）

猫の尻尾。（　しっぽ　）

竹刀を振る。（　しない　）

芝生に寝そべる。（　しばふ　）

雪崩が起こる。（　なだれ　）

叔父に会う。（　おじ　）

10

文章…小説や随筆、詩、手紙、電子メールなどの全体。

段落…文章の中で、まとまった内容を表すまとまり。段落の変わり目は行を改め、最初の一字分をあけて書く。

文……文章や段落の中で、一つのまとまった内容を表しているひとくぎり。文の終わりには、たいていの場合、「。」（句点）をつける。「?」（疑問符）や「!」（感嘆符）をつけることもある。

文章

文

段落　段落

文節……文を、実際に使われる表現として不自然にならないように、できるだけ細かくぎったひとまとまり。

＊文節に分けるときは、「ネ」や「ヨ」をつけてくぎるとよい。

例

今朝、／犬が／家の／庭を／ぐるぐる／走り回って／いた。
ネ　ネ　ネ　ネ　ネ　ネ

単語…文節を、意味をもつ最小の部分にくぎった、一つ一つの言葉。いくつかの単語が結びついてできた複合語は一単語として数える。

＊単語に分けるときは、文節ごとにくぎっていくとよい。

例

今朝、／犬｜が／家｜の／庭｜を／ぐるぐる／走り回っ｜て／い｜た。

複合語「走る」＋「回る」

文の成分には、次のものがある。

主語……「何（誰）」が」にあたる文節。

述語……「どうする」「どうである」「何だ」「ある・いる」などにあたる文節。

修飾語……「どんな」ものであるのかなどを詳しく述べる文節。修飾されるほうの文節は被修飾語という。

接続語…原因や理由などを表してあとの文節につながる文節。

独立語…他の文節とは直接にはつながらない文節。

例 ほら、晴れたら、空に にじが かかるよ。
（独立語／接続語／修飾語／主語／述語）

主語と述語との関係を主・述の関係、修飾語と被修飾語との関係を修飾・被修飾の関係という。
・「にじが」と「かかるよ」は、主・述の関係。
・「空に」と「かかるよ」は修飾・被修飾の関係。

文節の関係には、他に次のものがある。

並立の関係…二つ以上の文節が対等に並ぶ関係。

例 りんごや バナナは あまくて おいしい。

補助の関係…一方の文節が他方の実質的な意味を補助する関係。

例 考えて みると、その 方法は 難しくない。

連文節…二つ以上の文節がひとまとまりになって文の成分になるもの。

例 学校が 休みなので、（接続部／主・述の関係）
私と妹は、十時まで 寝て しまった。
（主部／並立の関係／修飾語／述部／補助の関係）

12

単語は、自立語と付属語に分けることができる。

自立語……それだけで文節をつくれる単語。

付属語……それだけでは文節をつくれず、必ず自立語につく単語。

さらに、単語は役割によって十種類に分けることができる。これを品詞という。

活用のない自立語

名詞……主語になることができる。（＝体言）

例 富士山、東京、彼、私、みかん、犬 など

連体詞……連体修飾語（＝体言を修飾する言葉）になる。

例 あらゆる 大きな たいした など

副詞……主に連用修飾語（＝用言を修飾する言葉）になる。

例 とても しばらく キラキラ など

接続詞……接続語になる。

例 そして だから など

感動詞……独立語になる。

例 ああ やあ など

活用のある自立語

動詞……ウ段の音で終わる。

例 歩く ある 来る する 見る など

形容詞……「い」で終わる。

例 近い おいしい 寒い 明るい など

形容動詞……「だ」「です」で終わる。

例 静かだ（です） きれいだ（です） など

活用のない付属語

助詞……言葉どうしの関係を示したり、いろいろな意味を添えたりする。

例 僕は兄と駅へ向かう。

活用のある付属語

助動詞……述語の意味を詳しくしたり、話し手の判断や気持ちを表したりする。

例 出かけたかったが、雨がやまないから、家にいよう。

▶ 漢字の知識

漢字の部首

偏（へん）…仕・校・持・性 にんべん てへん りっしんべん など

旁（つくり）…印・別・顔・戦 ふしづくり りっとう おおがい ほこづくり など

冠（かんむり）…安・空・第 うかんむり あなかんむり たけかんむり など

脚（あし）…兄・志・熱 ひとあし こころ れんが など

垂（たれ）…床・病 まだれ やまいだれ など

構（かまえ）…国・術 くにがまえ ゆきがまえ など

繞（にょう）…道・起 しんにょう そうにょう など

漢字の音と訓

音読み…中国での発音がもとになった「音」を表す読み方。

訓読み…漢字が日本で使われるときの「意味」を表す読み方。

重箱読み…音読み＋訓読みの熟語の読み方。

例 仕事（シ＋ごと） など

湯桶読み…訓読み＋音読みの熟語の読み方。

例 目線（め＋セン） など

熟語の構成

主語・述語 型…例 国営（国が営む）

修飾・被修飾語 型…例 激動（激しく動く）

述語・対象 型…例 読書（書を読む）

同類語 型…例 寒冷（寒い・冷たい）

反対語 型…例 上下（上・下）

接頭語 型…例 無理 不利 未知

接尾語 型…例 当然 詩的 油性

日本語の音声

音節…ひとまとまりの音。ほとんどは、子音と母音の組み合わせでできている。

- 清音　例「ア」「カ」「サ」など
- 濁音　例「ガ」「ブ」など
- 半濁音　例「パ」「プ」など
- 撥音　例「ン」
- 促音　例「ッ」
- 長音　例「ー」
- 拗音　例「キャ」「キュ」など

アクセント…言葉によってどこを高く、どこを低く発音するかという、音の高低のこと。

イントネーション…文を読むときの音の高低など、言葉のまとまり全体の調子のこと。

日本語の文字

表音文字…意味を表さず音だけを表す。

例　平仮名　片仮名　ローマ字

表意文字…音だけでなく意味も表す文字。

例　漢字

片仮名の成立

漢文を読む際の不便を解消するために、音を書き表す方法を工夫する中で、漢字の一部を切り取って片仮名が生まれた。

平仮名の成立

楷書は、日本語の文章を書き表すには不便だったので、行書や草書をもとに平仮名が生まれた。

方言と共通語

方言……地域によって違いがみられる言葉。単語や発音などに違いがある。

社会方言…所属する団体や世代などの社会的な原因で、違ってくる言葉。

共通語…昔の江戸周辺の地域使われていた言葉をもとに、近畿地方の方言などが加わってできた言葉。

ハ行

* 語中・語尾の「は」「ひ」「ふ」「へ」「ほ」
→「ワ」「イ」「ウ」「エ」「オ」

は	ひ	ふ	へ	ほ
わ	い	う	え	お
例 あはれ → アワレ	例 もの思ひ → モノオモイ	例 とふ → トウ	例 いへ → イエ	例 いとほし → イトオシ

ワ行

* 「ゐ」「ゑ」「を」→「イ」「エ」「オ」

ゐ	ゑ	を
い	え	お
例 ゐなか → イナカ	例 こゑ → コエ	例 をかし → オカシ

ダ行

* 「ぢ」「づ」→「ジ」「ズ」

ぢ	づ
じ	ず
例 もみぢ → モミジ	例 よろづ → ヨロズ

特別な読み

* 次のような母音（ぼいん）の連続は伸ばす音に

「ア段」+「う・ふ」→「オ段」の長音
「イ段」+「う・ふ」→「○ュウ」
「エ段」+「う・ふ」→「○ョウ」

au	iu	eu
ô	yû	yô
例 らうたし → ロウタシ	例 うつくしうて→ウツクシュウテ	例 てふてふ→チョウチョウ

* 次のような「む」「なむ」→「ン」「ナン」
例 戦はむ → タタカワン/竹なむ → タケナン

* 「くわ」「ぐわ」→「カ」「ガ」
例 くわんざし→カンザシ/ぐわんじつ→ガンジツ